Nick Vandome

Digital Photography for Seniors

For the Over 50s

second edition

In easy steps is an imprint of In Easy Steps Limited
Southfield Road · Southam
Warwickshire CV47 0FB · United Kingdom
www.ineasysteps.com

2nd Edition

Notice of Liability
Every effort has been made to ensure that this book contains accurate and current information. However, In Easy Steps Limited and the author shall not be liable for any loss or damage suffered by readers as a result of any information contained herein.

Trademarks
All trademarks are acknowledged as belonging to their respective companies.

Printed and bound in the United Kingdom

ISBN 978-1-84078-360-5

Contents

1 Joining the Digital Club

Everything is going digital and cameras are no exception. This chapter offers an introduction to digital photography.

Why this Book?

The expansion of digital photography has been remarkable: from being an expensive curiosity only a few years ago, it has now become the primary way in which people capture photographs. With this has come a similar growth in the number of books about digital photography. These cover a wide range of topics and most of them are aimed at all groups of users.

However, few books on digital photography concentrate specifically on the needs and requirements of seniors, who are perhaps new to the subject and all of its associated jargon and technology.

The aim of this book is to cut through some of the more complex areas of digital photography and focus on making the process of taking and using digital pictures as straightforward and satisfying as possible. With this in mind the book will cover many specific tasks connected with digital photography. These will include:

● Choosing the right digital camera, including issues such as the size of the camera and also the size of the camera's screen

● Taking better pictures, concentrating on popular areas such as holiday photographs and family shots

- The best and quickest ways to transfer digital photographs from a camera to a computer

- Simple editing techniques for quickly improving the appearance of digital photographs

- Sending and receiving digital photographs by email

- Sharing digital photographs on the Internet so that they can be viewed from locations worldwide

Don't forget

For further details of working with photo editing programs, see Chapter Eight.

Don't forget

For further details of using photos with email and on the Internet, see Chapters Nine and Ten.

- Printing and displaying photos so that you can make the most out of them once they have been taken

Don't forget

For further details of printing and displaying photos, see Chapters Eleven and Twelve.

Comparing Digital and Film

Although it sometimes seems that digital photography has its own complex and jargon-laden language, the good news is that the basic process of picture-taking is remarkably similar to that of taking pictures with a film camera.

Similarities

The similarities between taking pictures with digital and film cameras include:

- With both types of media the picture can be composed through the camera's viewfinder

- In most cases, the camera focuses the photo using autofocus. This is usually done by half-depressing the shutter release button until the photo is focused

- The photo is taken by fully depressing the camera's shutter release button

- The photo is captured by light passing through the camera's lens

Differences

Despite the similarities, there are also some differences when taking pictures with a digital camera:

- In addition to a traditional viewfinder, most digital cameras also have a screen on the back of the camera that can be used for composing pictures:

Hot tip

Look for a camera that has both a screen and a viewfinder, in case it is too sunny to see the screen properly.

- Once a photo is taken on a digital camera it is stored on a memory card within the camera, rather than on film. Memory cards come in a variety of sizes and can store a certain number of images, depending on their size. Once the memory card is full, the images can be downloaded onto a computer. After this, the images can be erased and the card used again. Think of a memory card as film that can be used over and over again

Some digital cameras also have internal memory for storing photos as well as using a memory card.

Don't forget

There are several different types of memory card on the market. However, you do not have to worry about what type is in your own camera as photos can be downloaded onto computers from all card types.

- Digital photos can be viewed as soon as they have been taken, using the camera's screen. If you want to, you can also delete photos from the memory card while it is in the camera. This can be done to get rid of unwanted images and free up space on the memory card

- Digital photos provide a lot more flexibility for use once they have been taken. They can be downloaded and edited on a computer, printed, emailed to family and friends around the world or shared on the World Wide Web

Don't forget

Memory cards have different capacities – which means they can store different numbers of photos. The capacity of memory cards is measured in megabytes or gigabytes. The larger the capacity, the more photos can be stored on the card.

Digital Jargon Explained

As with any form of new technology, digital photography has more than its fair share of jargon and acronyms:

- **Card reader**. This is a device that can be used to download photos from a memory card onto a computer. The card reader is connected to the computer via a cable. The memory card is then inserted into the card reader for downloading

- **Docking station**. This is another device for downloading photos. The camera is placed in the docking station and the downloading process commences automatically with the software provided. An excellent option for downloading photos with a minimum of fuss

- **Downloading**. The process of transferring photos from the camera to a computer or other device

- **Effective Pixel Count**. The actual number of pixels captured in a photo at the camera's highest setting

- **File size**. This is the size of a digital photo in terms of how much space it takes up on a memory card or a computer. Since digital photos are essentially just digital data they are measured in standard digital units, i.e. kilobytes or, more usually, megabytes. (Megabytes do not equate to megapixels)

- **Image sensor**. This is the device inside a digital camera that captures the light once it passes through the camera's lens. It then processes the data and passes it on to the camera's memory card. In some ways an image sensor is more like traditional film than the memory card is, even though it is not visible

- **Image size**. This is the physical size of the photo in terms of pixel dimensions, e.g. 3220 pixels x 2880 pixels. This size can be manipulated in a photo editing program

- **JPEG**. This is the most common file format for digital photos. JPEG stands for Joint Photographic Experts

Beware

Digital photos from different cameras can have different file sizes, even if they have the same number of pixels. This is because cameras can compress the pixels so that the final file sizes can vary considerably.

12

Don't forget

Image sensors come in two formats: CCD or CMOS. The majority of cameras use the CCD version.

Group and is usually identified by a .jpg extension at the end of a filename once the photo has been downloaded

- **Megapixel**. This is the term for a million pixels: e.g. 5 million pixels equals 5 megapixels

- **Memory card**. This is the card onto which photos are saved once the data has been captured by the image sensor. Memory cards are removable from the camera

- **Photo editing**. This is the process whereby digital photos are manipulated on a computer once they have been downloaded. There are numerous programs that can perform this task

- **Pixels**. The building blocks of digital photos. A pixel is a colored square that contains the digital data that helps make up the photo. The name is a contraction of Picture Element

- **Resampling**. This is the process whereby digital photos are made larger or smaller within photo editing software

- **Resolution**. A term used in a number of areas of digital photography. One definition refers to the size of a digital photo, e.g. a resolution of 6 megapixels. Another use for resolution refers to the way a photo can be manipulated to allow it to be displayed at different sizes. (For more information on this see Chapter Seven)

- **Uploading**. This is the process of copying photos held on your computer to another location. It is most commonly used in relation to online sharing and printing websites. If you want to use one of these services, you first have to upload your photos onto the site

- **Zoom (digital)**. This is a function of digital cameras whereby a subject is made bigger in the viewfinder or on the screen by increasing the size of the pixels

- **Zoom (optical)**. This is a more genuine zoom function as it makes the subject larger through the use of mirrors in the camera's lens

Don't forget

Since digital photos are just a collection of colored digital dots, it is possible to make them larger or smaller by adding or removing pixels from the photo.

Getting Enough Pixels

A common battle between digital camera manufacturers is what is known as the "pixel race". This is the continuing attempt to fit more and more pixels into each digital image.

Pixel is a contraction of Picture Element and pixels are the small colored squares that make up a digital photo. In general, the number of pixels in a digital image is counted in millions, or megapixels, e.g. 5 million pixels or 5 megapixels. When digital cameras are quoted as having a certain number of pixels or megapixels, this refers to the maximum number of pixels that the camera can capture in a single image. (However, this headline figure can sometimes be slightly misleading since some of the pixels are required for processing functions within the camera. The figure to look for to see the actual number of pixels in each image is known as the Effective Pixel Count and can be found in the manufacturer's specifications for the camera.)

The total number of pixels in a digital photo is calculated by multiplying the numbers for the width and height of the photo. So a photo that was 3000 pixels by 2000 pixels would have 6 million in total, or 6 megapixels.

In the early days of consumer digital cameras, 2 million pixels was considered a good value for a photo. Now, the bare minimum is 3 million pixels, with figures of 5, 6, 7 million and above becoming commonplace.

So why does it matter how many pixels are in a photo? The first thing to remember is that pixels can be captured at different qualities, so more does not necessarily equate to a better photo. Most digital cameras compress the photos to a certain degree, which involves discarding some of the unwanted digital data in each pixel. This helps to reduce the file size of each photo, even though it may still have a large number of pixels. As a rule, the more expensive the digital camera, the greater the quality of the pixels in each photo.

All things being equal though, the more pixels in a photo, the better the quality at which it can be printed. This is

Don't forget

Pixels in a digital photo are first captured on an image sensor within the camera before they are transferred to the camera's memory card. The quality of the image sensor can have more impact on the final quality of the image than the overall number of pixels.

14

because if there are more pixels then they can be packed more densely together and so blend into an overall image rather than appearing as individual colored blocks. If the pixels are visible it is known as a pixelated photo, which means that there are not enough pixels for it to be printed at a good quality at the selected print size.

15

Around the Camera

Much of the technical wizardry of a digital camera is hidden within the camera body. However, there are some important items that can be accessed externally:

Memory cards
These are inserted into a slot on the camera body. For more information about inserting memory cards, see Chapter Three.

Batteries
These are inserted in a similar way to memory cards. For more information about inserting batteries, see Chapter Three.

Camera to computer connection
Almost all digital cameras have a socket for a cable to be plugged in so that they can be connected to a computer. This can be used to download photos from the camera to the computer.

Camera to TV connection
A lot of digital cameras also have a connection for viewing photos directly on a television. The camera is connected to the television via a cable and then the photos on the camera can be viewed as a slide show:

Don't forget

For a detailed look at the controls on a digital camera, see Chapter Two, pages 28 and 29.

Hot tip

Viewing photos directly from the camera on a TV screen is a great way to have family slide shows, without first having to download photos onto a computer.

Expanding Your Horizons

Once you have taken a digital photo you can use it in the same way as one from a film camera: i.e. have it printed out. This can be done at home by downloading the photo onto a computer and printing it from there, or by taking the camera's memory card into a photographic retailer and asking them to print it directly from the card. Digital photos can be printed in the traditional fashion but also onto novelty items such as T-shirts, cakes and mugs.

Sharing by email

Digital photos can quickly and easily be attached to email and instantly sent to family and friends around the world.

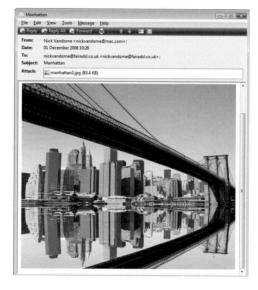

Beware

If you are sending digital photos by email, keep the file size relatively small so that they can be downloaded quickly. See Chapter Seven for details about making photos smaller.

Sharing on the Web

There are numerous sites on the Web where online photo albums can be created for sharing with family and friends:

...cont'd

Getting creative

Digital photos can also be incorporated into items such as cards and calendars, either by you, using a photo editing program, or through a photo retailer:

Beware

Online services charge a fee for creating items such as calendars and cards. However, you can do them yourself on a computer using a photo editing program (as with the sample on this page). For more details on this, see Chapter Twelve.

2 Choosing a Camera

This chapter looks at all the issues about getting the right camera for your needs, in terms of size, feel, screen and overall functionality.

The Right Camera Size

One aspect of all digital devices, from mobile phones to digital cameras, is that manufacturers are continually trying to make them smaller and smaller. For some groups of users this is a desirable design feature as they do not mind having a lot of small, fiddly buttons with which to operate devices. However, for senior users, something a bit more substantial is a definite advantage as it is easier to hold steady and the controls are more accessible.

When you are looking for a digital camera it is important to find one that is not too small. There are a number of disadvantages to smaller cameras:

- It can be hard to keep the camera steady when taking photos as there is not enough of it to hold on to

- The controls can be difficult to access and operate

- The lens and flash can be more easily obscured when taking photos

In general, look for a digital camera that is fairly solid and has a comfortable feel to it when you are holding it. For this reason, it is important to physically try a camera before you buy it. Sometimes cameras look suitable but they just don't feel right in your hands. From the front, the camera should look as if it will be easy to hold comfortably:

Hot tip

Take some photos with any cameras that you try, so that you can get a feel for them in a proper photo-taking situation.

From the back, the controls should be well placed, with enough room between them:

Don't forget

The controls on a digital camera are usually situated on the top and back of the camera body.

Beware

Smaller cameras, with no grip, can be harder to hold comfortably and operate efficiently. They are also more likely to get lost.

21

Camera grip

Larger digital cameras tend to have a much more solid camera grip. This is the side of the camera held by the right hand and it can be an excellent way to keep the camera steady. Look for a camera grip that has a rubber surface, as this provides extra stability.

Looking for a Large Screen

When digital cameras first came onto the market, one of their most revolutionary features was the screen at the back of the camera. This is known as the LCD (Liquid Crystal Display) screen and it serves a dual purpose: it can be used to frame and compose photos instead of the viewfinder and it can also be used to view, or delete, photos once they have been taken.

LCD screens continue to be a vital element of digital cameras and one welcome development in recent years has been that their size has increased significantly. When looking at a digital camera, always try and find one that has a large screen (a minimum of 2 inches across). This will make it easier both for composing photos and for viewing them once they have been taken.

Beware

A few cheaper digital cameras do not have a screen, but these should be avoided.

Hot tip

Test a camera's screen in direct sunlight to see how clear, or otherwise, it is.

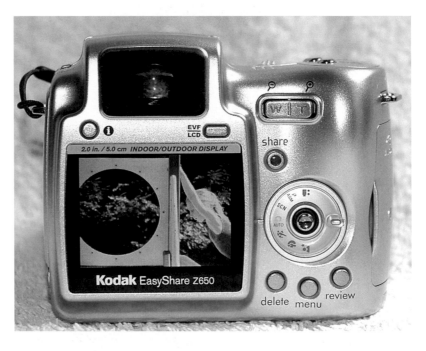

Using a viewfinder

Although a large screen is a definite advantage, there is one situation where it can be a distinct disadvantage. This is when the screen is so large that it takes up the whole of the back of the camera and there is no space for a traditional viewfinder. This is fine, unless you are trying to take photos in very bright or sunny conditions, in which case the glare from the sun may make it very hard to see what is on the screen. Because of this it is important to have a traditional viewfinder too, in case the screen cannot be used properly.

Look for a screen and viewfinder together:

Hot tip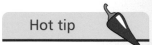

Look for a viewfinder that has a rubber edge surrounding it. This will make it more comfortable and easier to look through.

23

Switching between screen and viewfinder

If a camera has a screen and a viewfinder it is only possible to use one of them at a time. To switch between the two there will be a button on the back of the camera that can be pressed to toggle between screen and viewfinder as required.

Benefits of Docking Stations

An important part of digital photography is getting the photos from the camera onto a computer so that they can then be edited, emailed and shared online. There are three main ways of doing this:

- Connecting the camera directly to the computer

- Removing the camera's memory card and putting it into a card reader that is connected to the computer

- Using a docking station

All of these methods are looked at in detail in Chapter Six, but serious consideration should be given to using a docking station, as this is the quickest method and involves the least effort with connecting cables or removing and inserting memory cards.

A docking station is a device that connects the camera to the computer. The docking station only has to be connected to the computer once, and then the camera can be placed in the docking station whenever you want to download photos:

Don't forget

A range of Kodak cameras come with docking stations and also dedicated printers that can act as a docking station.

Advantages

There are a number of advantages to using a docking station:

- Ease of use. Photos can be downloaded by placing the camera on the docking station and pressing a single button

- Software provided. Docking stations come supplied with compatible software. When the camera is placed on the docking station, the software recognizes it and launches automatically

Beware

Docking stations have to be used with the software provided in order to download photos from the camera to the computer.

25

- Recharging. In addition to downloading photos, docking stations also charge the camera's batteries, so you do not have to worry about a separate charger for rechargeable batteries

Not all digital camera makers provide docking stations for their cameras. Kodak are the main manufacturer of cameras with compatible docking stations and they also provide their own Easyshare software to use with these devices. This provides the means to download photos using the docking station and it also provides an environment for editing and organizing the photos once they have been downloaded.

Don't forget

Kodak digital cameras that use docking stations have an instant sharing facility for emailing images or sharing with other people over the Web.

Up Close with Zoom

Most compact digital cameras now have some form of zoom capability. This is a fairly essential feature as it enables you to make the subject of a photo appear larger without having to get closer to it. This can be useful in a number of situations:

- **Portraits**. Zoom can be used to fill the frame with the subject, without you having to get too close and crowd them. This will make the subject feel more relaxed

- **Candid shots**. These benefit from the use of zoom as it enables you to take photos of people when they are engaged in activities without them being aware of the presence of the camera. It is particularly effective with children

- **Buildings**. Details of buildings and architecture can be picked out through the use of zoom

- **Animals**. Frequently, photos of animals are disappointing as the subjects appear too small. A large zoom facility can help to solve this problem

Types of zoom

When looking at digital cameras you will be quoted two different figures, one for optical zoom and one for digital zoom. Of the two, optical zoom is much more important as it physically moves the lens's mirrors within the camera to make the subject appear larger. Digital zoom just enlarges the photo on the screen or in the viewfinder. In general, ignore the digital zoom figure and concentrate on the size of the optical zoom.

Accessing zoom

On most cameras, there is a button for accessing the zoom function. Press W (-) to give a wide-angle shot and T (+) for a telephoto shot (one where the subject appears closer).

Wide angle

Use wide angle when you want to get as much of a scene in the photo as possible:

Telephoto

Use telephoto when you want to get close to a subject and make it look as large as possible:

Hot tip

It is always worth taking two photos of the same scene, one with the least amount of zoom and one with greatest amount of zoom. This can produce dramatically different results.

Around the Controls

Although different digital cameras will have their controls in slightly different places, most of them have very similar sets of controls to give the camera its functionality:

On-off
The on-off button is used to power the camera on and off. It usually has two options: one for accessing the photo-taking functions of the camera and one for the viewing and reviewing of photos.

Shutter release button
This is almost always situated on the top of the camera and is used to focus a photo and then capture it.

Zoom controls
As shown on the previous two pages, these are used to zoom in to, or out from, subjects in a photo.

Flash
There is usually a button to activate the flash and also a button to scroll through the options for flash, such as red-eye reduction or turning the flash off completely.

Landscape or close-up
This button can be used to specify whether you are taking a distant shot or a close-up one. If these options are selected, the camera will make the appropriate settings automatically.

Self-timer
This is usually used if you want to include yourself in a photo and need a few seconds to move into the shot.

Delete

This can be used to delete photos immediately after they have been taken. It can also be used to delete photos when they are being viewed using the camera's review function.

Menu

This can be used to access the relevant menus for the current function. For instance, if you are in photo-taking mode, the menus will apply to taking photos, and if you are in review mode they will give review options.

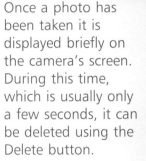

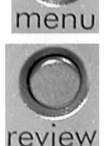

Don't forget

Once a photo has been taken it is displayed briefly on the camera's screen. During this time, which is usually only a few seconds, it can be deleted using the Delete button.

Review

This is used to view photos that have already been taken. It can be accessed at any time.

Camera controls

These are controls that determine the functionality of the camera. Some of the most common are:

- Auto, when the camera selects all of the settings

- Scene, when preset selections can be made for different photographic situations

Don't forget

Aperture priority mode is usually denoted by an A on the camera controls and shutter speed priority is denoted by an S.

- Aperture priority or shutter speed priority. This can be used by more experienced photographers if they want to set the aperture or shutter speed of the camera

- Video, which allows for short videos to be taken

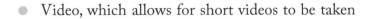

Setting up the Camera

Sometimes photography is a nice leisurely pastime: a landmark or landscape is well positioned in front of you and you have plenty of time to take the photo. However, more often than not there will be a certain degree of time constraint when taking a photo: a grandchild may be playing a game or activity that needs to be captured quickly; a sunset could be vanishing in a matter of moments; or you may want to get a photo of a fast-moving vehicle or animal. With all of these examples it is important to have the camera ready for use as quickly as possible. This means that if there are any settings that you want to specify, these should already be done before you are ready to take photos. If not, you may end up fiddling with the settings and then miss the vital picture. In most cases, it is perfectly acceptable to leave the camera on Auto, in which case it will take care of all of the picture-taking settings. However, there may be times when you want to change some of the settings manually. If you are doing this, think about the types of photos that you are going to be taking and then make the relevant settings before you start the photo-taking process. Some settings that you might want to consider changing are:

Hot tip

For more advanced functions, such as aperture and shutter speed priority, there are more settings that you can change manually.

- **Picture size**. This is the size, in pixels, at which the photo will be captured. This will normally be shown as a megapixel size, e.g. 6 megapixels. There will be a number of different settings for this on your camera, which can be accessed from the camera's menu system. As a general rule, use the largest picture size for photos that you want to use for printing and a smaller one for photos that you are going to email or use on the Web

- **Color**. This will enable you to determine the color of the photo. The options range from natural and bright colors, to sepia and black & white

- **Autofocus**. This determines how the autofocus works. The options are usually single, in which case the autofocus only works when the shutter release button is half depressed, or continuous, in which case the camera tries to autofocus continuously

Using the Camera's Scenes

A common feature on a lot of digital cameras is a choice of scene modes. These are modes that have assigned settings for specific photographic situations. So, if you are taking photos at night and are unsure of the settings to use, you could use the Night scene to simplify the process greatly.

If a camera has scene modes it will probably have quite a few of them. Some of the most common are:

- **Children mode**. For capturing action photos of children in bright light

- **Sport mode**. For capturing fast-moving action, such as sporting events

- **Portrait mode**. For capturing portraits against a softened background

- **Landscape mode**. For capturing landscapes in vivid colors. In landscape mode the focus is set to infinity

- **Fireworks mode**. This uses a slow shutter speed to capture the effect of fireworks at night. A tripod is essential for this type of shot as it will result in a blurred photo otherwise

...cont'd

- **Backlight mode**. This can be used where the main subject is in front of a brightly lit area. In this mode, the flash will fire automatically to illuminate the main subject and so equalize its lighting with the brighter background

- **Close-up mode**. For capturing photos at very short distances. Usually used for small objects

- **Snow mode**. This can be used when capturing photos in very bright conditions. In this mode, the lighting of the brightly lit areas will be exposed accurately without altering the exposure of any other objects in the photo

Don't forget

Always use a tripod if you are going to be taking photos at night or indoors without the use of flash.

- **Night modes**. There are usually a couple of night modes, one for landscapes and one for portraits. For both of these a tripod is essential to keep the camera steady

- **Museum mode**. For capturing photos when you do not want the camera to make any noise, and you do not want the flash to fire. It can be used in locations such as museums or at indoor events such as school plays

3 Getting up and Running

This chapter deals with what happens when you first start using a digital camera. It covers some of the accessories you need and shows how to take and view your first photos, and delete any you don't want.

Inserting a Memory Card

Memory cards are vital elements in the digital photography process. These are removable cards that are inserted into a digital camera and used to store photos once they are captured. Memory cards come in a variety of types but the good news is that you do not have to worry about the type of card that comes with your camera, as photos can be downloaded or printed from any type of memory card. When using a digital camera it is important to know how to insert, and remove, the memory card:

34

1 To insert a memory card, open its compartment cover on the camera

2 Push in the memory card until it clicks into place. Do not force it in

3 To remove the memory card, press the button next to the card, or press the memory card itself until it pops out

Inserting Batteries

Digital cameras use a lot of battery power so it is best to choose a camera that uses some form of rechargeable batteries. Some cameras use traditional batteries that can be recharged with a battery charger, and others take solid lithium battery packs. Either type of rechargeable battery must be charged and inserted into the camera. To do this:

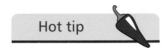
Hot tip

If possible, use a camera with rechargeable lithium batteries.

1 Insert the battery, or batteries, into the charger and wait until they are fully charged

2 Open the battery compartment cover on the camera (in some cases this may be the same compartment that holds the memory card)

Hot tip

Always carry a spare, fully charged, battery with you whenever you are taking photos.

3 Insert the battery, or batteries, according to the diagram on the battery compartment

4 Close the battery compartment cover firmly

Turning the Camera on

Once the memory card and charged batteries have been inserted it is time to turn the camera on. This activates the camera's digital circuitry and prepares it for use. To do this:

1 Before use, the camera lens will be retracted

2 Press the Power button on, or move it to the on position (It is usually located on the top or back of the camera)

3 The camera will make some whirring and clicking sounds as it prepares itself for use

4 The lens will be opened and, in some cases, extended

5 The screen at the back of the camera will be activated and display the view through the lens

Keeping the Camera Steady

One problem in all forms of photography is an effect called camera shake. This is where a small amount of hand movement when a photo is being taken causes the camera to shake slightly, resulting in a fuzzy and out of focus photo. There are a number of ways to try and keep the camera as steady as possible and avoid camera shake:

1 Use a full length tripod. This is the best option for keeping the camera steady, but it can be cumbersome to carry around all the time

2 Use a mini-tripod. These can be bought at camera shops and are an excellent compromise between size and steadiness. They fit easily into a pocket

3 A small bean bag. This can be used instead of a tripod to steady the camera

Hot tip

When looking at a tripod, make sure it has a good sturdy head that can hold the camera firmly in position at all times.

Don't forget

Mini-tripods are usually about six inches in height and have pliable legs that can be bent into place.

...cont'd

4 A shoulder bag. Small bags can also be used in a similar way to a bean bag, depending what you are carrying in your bag

5 Benches or barriers. These can be used to give extra stability when taking photos:

6 Doorframes or pillars. This is another option for achieving greater stability when you are hand-holding the camera while you are taking a photo:

Beware

Although benches and doorframes can give additional stability, they will not be enough to avoid camera shake in low-level lighting, such as at night.

Taking Your First Shot

With the camera turned on, and steady, you are ready to take your first shot. To do this:

1 Position the camera so that you can see clearly through the screen to compose the photo

39

Hot tip

Before you start taking photos, read the camera's manual as this will provide useful technical and picture-taking information.

2 Compose the scene and half-depress the shutter release button to focus the shot, using the camera's autofocus. A light should appear on the screen when the shot is in focus

3 Keep the shutter release button half depressed once focus has been achieved

4 Fully depress the shutter release button to take the photo

5 The photo will be visible on the screen

Don't forget

Since you are not using up any film you can experiment extensively when you first get a digital camera and take as many shots as you like.

Getting the Timing Right

One ongoing issue when taking photos with a digital camera is a problem known as time lag. There are three types of time lag and they all affect the timing when taking digital photos.

Start-up time lag

This is the time that it takes a digital camera to be ready for use when it is turned on. Due to the amount of digital processing that goes on within the camera, the start-up time can be a few seconds. Obviously this can have an impact on capturing certain types of photos if your camera is not ready.

Shot time lag

This is the amount of time that it takes for a photo to be captured once the shutter release button has been pressed. This is usually only fractions of a second but it can have a significant impact on photos of moving objects or people, especially children, particularly if they move or blink just as the photo is being taken, resulting in an unflattering pose:

Recycling time lag

This is the amount of time it takes the camera to get ready for the next shot. When a photo is taken the camera has to process the information and copy it to the memory card. Depending on the efficiency of the camera this can take a few seconds. While this is happening the camera will lock and not allow you to take another photo.

Hot tip

Most digital cameras have details in their technical specifications of the amount of time lag. If you know the shot time lag then you can sometimes adjust the shot accordingly.

Reducing time lag

Although time lag cannot be removed completely, there are a number of ways to minimize its effects:

1 Keeping your camera turned on all the time. Most cameras have a Sleep mode that will save battery power but still allow the camera to be turned on. Although there is still a slight time lag when Sleep mode is deactivated, this is not as long as the time lag for turning the camera on

2 Take several consecutive shots of a subject. This is particularly important for photos of subjects such as grandchildren as they are likely to make sudden movements. This can be done with the camera's Burst function, if it has one, where several photos can be taken consecutively while the shutter release button is still depressed:

Beware

Burst functions can use up a lot more battery power than capturing photos individually.

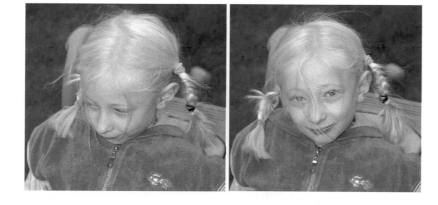

3 Use a good quality memory card. Memory cards copy digital data at different speeds and the faster the information is copied the quicker it is ready for the next shot. In general, the more expensive the memory card the quicker it will be

Looking at Photos

As soon as photos have been taken it is possible to view them on the camera. This is an invaluable way to see how the photo has turned out and if any adjustments are required. To review photos:

1 Press the Review button on the camera

2 Photos can be viewed on the camera's screen

3 Use the zoom function on the camera to get a close-up view of parts of the photo

4 Use the buttons on the back of the camera to move through the photos that have been taken

Deleting Photos

One of the great advantages of digital photography is that you can delete any photos that you do not like, directly from the camera. This can be done when a photo has just been taken or while they are being reviewed. To do this:

1 Immediately after a photo has been taken it will be displayed briefly on the camera's screen. If you do not want to keep it press the Delete button, or

2 Select the Review function on the camera and select a photo you want to delete

3 Press the Delete button

4 In the Delete Confirmation window, select Picture to delete the photo

Don't forget

The procedure for deleting photos can vary in detail from camera to camera, but the general approach is always the same.

Beware

Most delete functions have an option for deleting all photos stored in the camera or on the memory card. If you select this option, make sure the photos have already been downloaded or that you definitely do not want them.

Keeping Your Camera Safe

Although digital cameras are relatively robust externally, they have a number of delicate elements within them so it is best to try and keep them as safe as possible. To do this:

1. Buy a case for the camera to keep it safe when not in use. Make sure this fits the camera securely

2. Always use the neck strap when using the camera:

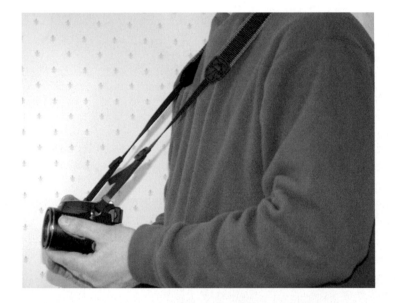

3. Keep the camera away from water. Water is one of the biggest threats to digital cameras so always try and keep them out of the rain and away from areas of water such as the sea or swimming pools. If your camera does get wet, try and dry it out completely before you use it again

4. If you are on holiday with your digital camera, keep it out of sight as much as possible, particularly in poorer countries where it may be considered an item of considerable worth

(4) Family and Friends

Photos of family and friends are always popular. This chapter shows how to get the most out of this subject and how to improve your photos of people in different situations.

Using Screen and Viewfinder

Taking photos of family and friends is one of the most common, and most satisfying, uses for a digital camera. One of the great advantages is that everyone can see the photos immediately afterwards and several photos can be taken at one time, if required.

When capturing photos of family and friends there may be occasions when you want to switch between using the camera's screen and its viewfinder:

1 Use the camera's screen when capturing groups of people. This will enable you to look at them directly and talk to them in a more natural fashion while you are still composing the photo with the screen:

2 Use the viewfinder if it is important to keep the camera as steady as possible, such as for individual portraits. This is because if you use the screen the camera is further away from your body and so does not have as much support

Positioning Family Groups

When taking photos of family groups it is sometimes hard to get everyone together at the same time. However, if you manage to do this it can be beneficial to take some extra time and deliberately position family members so that the group composition is more interesting. Two possible ways to do this are:

1 Arrange people in a variety of positions – some standing, sitting, lying, or in more acrobatic poses (use the younger, more flexible family members for the more difficult poses!)

Hot tip

When capturing photos of family groups you sometimes have to be a bit bossy in order to get everyone in the positions that you require.

47

2 Arrange the group around existing objects. These can be constructed or naturally occurring. Either way, it will add an extra dimension to the family group. This is a useful technique for photos of individuals as well as groups

Including Yourself

In a lot of family group shots there is usually one person missing: the photographer. At times when families are together it is important to include everyone who is there. If you are taking the photo, it is still possible to include yourself in the picture. To do this:

Set up the camera on a tripod

2 Arrange the group as you want them. Leave a space somewhere for yourself. Take a couple of test shots to make sure that there is enough space

Hot tip

If you are including yourself in a photo outdoors you can stand the camera on an object such as a rock if you do not have a tripod available.

48

3 Access the camera's self timer, by pressing this button:

4 Half-depress the shutter release button to focus the camera

5 Fully depress the shutter release button to activate the self timer

6 The camera will flash during the period of the self timer. This means that the photo has not yet been taken. This should give you enough time to position yourself in the shot

7 After a set period of time (usually about 20 seconds) the self timer will take the photo

Beware

If you are including yourself in a group that includes children there is the chance that they may move while waiting for the self timer to work.

49

8 If you do not think you will have time to get into position, compose the photo with yourself in it and get someone else to activate the camera

Removing Shadows

When taking photos of family and friends on a bright, sunny day it is easy to think that you have the perfect conditions. However, a problem can occur – people may appear shaded despite the fact that it is sunny. This happens when the sun is behind them, causing their fronts to be in shadow. This can be rectified through the use of flash:

50

1   If you capture a photo of someone with the sun behind them, they will appear in shadow

2   Turn on your camera's flash and take the photo again

3   The flash lightens up the front of the subjects, giving a much more balanced effect with the bright, sunny background

Family Occasions

At family occasions such as weddings, parties and anniversaries there are usually a significant number of other family members who are taking photographs. At times like this it can be a good idea to try and capture candid shots to supplement the more formal photos that will be taken.

1. Use a large zoom setting to capture photos without people realizing that you are taking their picture. This can result in a much more natural pose

2. Capture photos of people's reactions to things, such as when chatting informally at a party:

3. Keep your camera at your side and take photos from this angle. This will capture candid shots and also add a different perspective to the photos

Hot tip

If there is a professional photographer at a family occasion, position yourself near to them so that you can get some photos using their compositions. You can also ask them to take a photo with your camera so that you can be included in the photo too.

51

Photos of Grandchildren

Grandchildren can be the most satisfying of photographic subjects and also one of the most frustrating. This is because children tend to keep moving constantly and they do not always want to keep still for photographs. However, there are a number of techniques that can be deployed to try and get better pictures of grandchildren:

1 Give them something to hold on to while you are taking their photo. This will help distract their attention from posing for the photo

Don't forget

Using zoom also helps to blur the background, which is a good effect in photos of children.

2 Use the zoom to get a close-up shot, without having to get too physically close to them

3   Photograph them when they are involved in some
    form of activity, so that they are less aware of the
    camera's presence

4   Let your grandchildren take photos of each other.
    This may lead to surprisingly good results

Hot tip

Even young children
are very technologically
aware these days and
may even be able to
offer advice about the
workings of digital
cameras.

53

Portraits

Portraits of individual family members make great photographs for displaying on walls or mantelpieces. In some cases these can be taken by professional photographers, but this can be expensive. Alternatively, it is perfectly possible to take your own high-quality photos of other family members. To do this:

1. Give the person plenty of warning about the photo. This will enable them to prepare themselves

2. Select a suitable location, with an attractive background

3. Take a standard shot to begin with. This may be an interesting shot in its own right, but the attention is as much on the background as the main subject

4. To give more prominence to the main subject, they should fill the frame more and the background should be less defined

Hot tip

Portrait shots can always be cropped in photo editing software to make the subject fill the frame more fully. Because of this it is important to take portrait shots with the highest resolution setting (maximum number of pixels) on the camera.

5   Move the subject further away from the background

6   Use the maximum zoom setting to zoom in on the subject. If necessary, move further back to fit in the subject once the zoom is fully extended

Hot tip

If your camera has an aperture priority mode (A) this can be used to make the background even blurrier. To do this, set the aperture to its widest setting (i.e. its lowest f-number) and this will have the effect of throwing the background even more out of focus.

7   The high degree of zoom and larger distance between the subject and the background has the effect of throwing the background out of focus, giving more attention to the subject

Filling the Frame

One technique for capturing portraits is to fill the frame with as much of the subject's face as possible. This can create a very powerful effect since every feature of the face is detailed in the image. This type of image is frequently used for politicians and business people as it conveys a sense of control and it can also look slightly intimidating. However, it is also a productive technique for photos of family and friends as it can create a more intimate portrait.

When capturing this type of image it is vital to use a zoom lens and the bigger the better. To create the same effect without a zoom would result in you being only inches away from the subject's face, which is unlikely to result in a natural-looking image.

A shot without the zoom can create a perfectly acceptable photo but is more of a snapshot than a portrait.

Instead, take a shot where the whole face fills the viewfinder or the LCD panel. This creates a much more intimate effect and you can start to really see the character of the subject.

Another option for this type of image is to convert it to black and white once it has been captured. This can either be done through the camera's menu system or in a photo editing program. A black and white portrait adds an extra dimension to a subject.

Eliminating Red-eye

Red-eye is a common photographic problem, caused when taking photos with the flash. When the flash is used, it reflects in the retina of the subject's eye, causing the red-eye effect. There are a number of ways to try and avoid or remove red-eye:

Beware

The red-eye reduction function on a digital camera can be disconcerting due to the double flash that occurs. If you are comfortable editing photos on the computer then this can be a better option for reducing red-eye.

1 Use the camera's red-eye reduction function. Most digital cameras have this and it works by firing an additional flash, just before the photo, with the main flash, is taken. This has the effect of reducing the reflection when the photo is taken

2 Move the subject so that they are not directly in front of the camera

3 Use a photo editing program to remove red-eye from the photo on a computer. This is a simple process and one that is available in most photo editing programs. This is usually a one- or two- step operation. It involves zooming in on the affected area and then selecting the relevant red-eye removal tool. The red-eye can then be removed by clicking on the affected area or by dragging around it with the red-eye tool

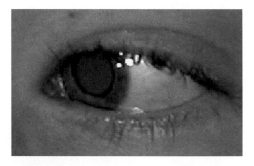

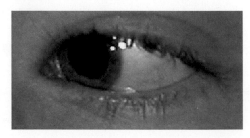

5 Better Holiday Photos

This chapter offers some straightforward techniques that can be used to turn basic holiday snaps into quality photos, including photos of wildlife and night photos.

Improving Holiday Snaps

When on holiday or traveling there are usually numerous excellent photographic opportunities. However, a lot of these opportunities can be wasted through a lack of care or attention, or the thought that "it's only a holiday snap." Through spending a little more time on each photo and employing some simple techniques it is possible to turn throwaway holiday snaps into impressive photographs.

Composing accurately

One of the most simple mistakes made when composing photos is that they are not positioned accurately. This can lead to parts of the image being cut off when the photo is captured.

To solve this problem, make sure there is a reasonable border around the main subject when you view it with the camera's screen or viewfinder. If you are using zoom, reduce the level of zoom slightly so that there is enough of a border.

Being patient

When capturing holiday snaps, it can be tempting to take a lot of photos quickly, without thinking too much about them. However, it can pay great dividends to be patient and take a bit of time over each shot. This could be something as simple as waiting for someone to move out of the way of the shot or until the sun comes out from behind a cloud:

Hot tip

Checking the daily weather forecast can give you important information that can be used for your photographic activities while on holiday.

...cont'd

Two-line grid

When taking photos on holiday, the natural temptation is to position the main subject in the middle of the shot. While this creates a perfectly acceptable photo, it is possible to move the main subject to create a more interesting composition. One way to do this is by using a two-line grid. To do this, imagine two horizontal lines across the image and position the horizon at a different line in each shot. In the photo below the main subject is positioned in the lower/middle third of the frame, rather than directly in the middle. This gives it more balance as it includes more of the sky behind the subject.

Don't forget

Moving the camera up or down a couple of inches can have a dramatic impact on the final photos and it is always worth trying.

In this photo the main subject is positioned at the top of the frame i.e. at the top line of the grid. This creates a very evocative image as the foreground can then be used to great effect. In this case the presence of the two individuals gives the photo much more depth as the building is not the only element to which the eye is drawn.

Don't forget

Sometimes the best shot is with the main subject in the center of a photo, so make sure you always take some like this too.

...cont'd

Four-line grid

Once you have mastered using a two-line grid for composing photos, you can then move on to a four-line grid. This is similar in theory but it gives more flexibility for positioning subjects within the photo, as the photo is then divided into nine sections and the main subject can be positioned in any of the sections: In the two images below, the main element has been placed along the left and right-hand vertical lines in the grid, both achieving different effects and photos.

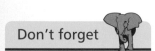

Don't forget

A four-line grid consists of two horizontal lines and two vertical lines.

Don't forget

Do not be too strict in your use of grids. Sometimes a good eye for a photo can mean more than technical considerations.

In this photo the main subject is positioned in the center of the grid. Because of its size this draws the eye through the whole center column of the image, creating a very powerful and effective photo.

Photographing Landmarks

When on holiday some of the main photographic subjects are the local landmarks. This can be one of the most rewarding areas of photography, but some creative thought should go into the process to try and get as good a picture as possible:

1 Capturing a standard, straightforward photo of a landmark is perfectly acceptable

2 Include other objects in the photo to give it an extra dimension

Don't forget

Most famous landmarks are illuminated at night and this can provide some excellent photographic opportunities. However, make sure you use a tripod, since the camera's flash will not be powerful enough.

...cont'd

3 Use the zoom or move in close to get some photos of the detail of a landmark. This gives a landmark a sense of individuality. It is also a good way to give more meaning to your vacation photos: rather than dozens of standard photos of landmarks, some shots of the detail will help create more contrast

4 Capture a landmark in unusual conditions, such as stormy weather or at night. For night shots, turn off the camera's flash and use a tripod so that the shutter speed of the camera can capture the required elements of the image

Hot tip

Car tail lights can create very effective and artistic streaks when taking night photos. To do this, set the camera to Shutter Speed priority (S) and use a shutter speed of 1 second or more. This will create the streaks of light as the cars pass by the camera.

Camera Orientation

Taking good photographs does not have to involve large amounts of high-tech, expensive equipment. In a lot of cases a good eye for a photograph can be more important than the equipment being used. Part of this involves changing the angle at which an image is being viewed. There are a number of ways in which this can be achieved, but the simplest is to change the camera's orientation. This is a case of rotating the camera by 90 degrees so that the image is captured in portrait rather than landscape.

Even if you have taken one good photograph, this simple technique of changing the orientation can ensure that you have another impressive shot, which shows the subject from a different perspective. Since you are not using up any film it is always worthwhile to take shots with different orientations so that you can compare them at a later date. Also, if you want to crop the image you will have more scope to do this if you have the main subject in different orientations.

This shot in landscape is a good way to capture the whole width of the detailed towers.

In this portrait shot the full scale of the structure can
be appreciated. When taking photos of buildings always
envisage how they will look in both portrait and landscape.

Standing Out

When on vacation a good way to see a city or location is to take a tour on a bus or coach. This is ideal for sightseeing but it can be a drawback when it comes to taking photos. This is because all of the buses and coaches usually stop in the same place so you will end up taking photos in among a crowd of people and vehicles.

If you want to stand out from the crowd and take more unusual photos, a bit of effort is required. This means moving to a different location to take your photos. Move further away from the main subject so that the tourist buses and coaches are not visible. Depending on the distance, you may have to zoom in on the subject in order to fill the screen sufficiently.

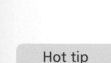

Hot tip

When taking photos on holiday, try thinking of yourself as a photographer rather than a tourist.

Another option for making a vacation photo stand out is to capture the subject from a different angle. This can involve trying to get above the subject so that you are looking down on it rather than being at the same level. Hills are an obvious option for this type of shot, but you could also use cable cars or take shots through the windows of planes.

...cont'd

If you can't capture your subject from an unusual angle then you can try and make it stand out in the editing process. To do this, take a standard photo of a landmark:

Don't forget

For more information about creating artistic effects, and photo editing in general, see Chapter Eight.

In a program such as Photoshop Elements, special effects can be applied to create dozens of artistic effects that can help your photos really stand out.

Wildlife

Photographing wildlife can be a challenge, but a very rewarding one if you get it right. The key to this type of photography is preparation, patience and getting close enough. Here are some steps to follow:

1 Before you start, make sure that your camera is working, there is enough room on the memory card and the batteries are fully charged

2 When you get to your location take some time to blend in with the surroundings so that the animals become used to you. This could just involve sitting still, or stopping a vehicle on a safari

3 If your zoom is too small the wildlife will look like a speck in the distance

4 Use the maximum optical zoom available to make the animals appear as large as possible

5 Never be afraid to take what you may think are clichéd photos of animals. If you are actually there these can turn out to be some of the most dramatic and cherished photos that you will ever take (for the type of photo below a good zoom lens is advisable, so that you don't have to be too close to the subject!)

Hot tip

If you are on a once-in-a-lifetime trip, such as a safari, make sure that you have spare, fully charged, batteries and a spare memory card. Take memory cards that can store as many photos as possible.

6 As well as animals, birds are another rich source for photos. If you can get close enough they provide limitless opportunities for photos displaying their character and humor

Using Sunlight

Natural sunlight is one of the best conditions under which to take photos. However, taking photos in strong sunlight, such as at midday, does not always produce the best results. This is because the light is too strong and harsh and it does not bring the maximum amount of color from a subject.

To make the best use of sunlight, photos should ideally be taken during the hour after dawn and the hour before sunset. This is when the light is not directly overhead and it creates a much richer, softer type of lighting and color. This is known as the Golden Hour and it is a time during which some excellent photos can be taken:

1 In direct sunlight a subject can appear slightly harsh with too little contrast

2 If the shot is taken during the Golden Hour, the color will be much more satisfying

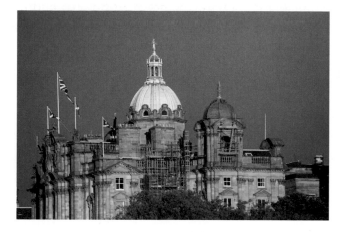

3 The Golden Hour can be used to capture some very atmospheric photos

4 Sunsets can be very dramatic and this can be a good opportunity for creating silhouettes

Hot tip

To create silhouettes, keep the sunset in the middle of the photo. This will ensure the photo is exposed correctly for the sunset, thus ensuring the buildings are underexposed, i.e. very dark or black.

Storytelling

Some photographic locations offer the chance for one single, stunning photo. However, in most cases, there are numerous opportunities for capturing a variety of photos. Even if you cannot immediately see the chance for different photos it is always worthwhile looking around a location to see if you can capture a range of shots. Start with some standard shots, but make sure you capture the subject in different lighting conditions and times of day.

Hot tip

Spend plenty of time at a particular location. This will allow you to get a feel for it during different times of the day and in different lighting conditions.

Find areas of detail that help to give a deeper understanding of the subject and show its true character. This can include building details, paintings, tapestries or mosaics. This is also a good discipline to get into as it helps you look in greater detail at whichever location you are at.

Try and find some elements that add local color or humor to the location.

Don't forget

Photos that are captured as part of a story can make for much more interesting slide shows than dozens of standard shots of a location.

Finally, make sure that you take some photos at dusk to get sunsets and silhouettes.

Night Photos

Taking photos at night can produce some dramatic results and it should always be an option, particularly when on vacation. The essential thing to remember if you are taking photos of sunsets, landscapes or landmarks is not to use the flash, since it will not be powerful enough to light up the scene. Instead, the camera should be put on a tripod while the photo is being taken. This is because the camera's shutter will need to be open for several seconds to allow enough light to pass into the camera. If it was being hand-held then the camera would shake and the photo would be blurred. Using a tripod requires a bit more effort but the results can be worth it:

Hot tip

Try and include objects or people within sunsets, as this makes for a much more interesting photo.

...cont'd

The evening or dusk is also a great time to capture silhouettes of people. To do this, keep the flash on your camera turned off and point the camera at the area of light created by the setting sun (or in the bottom image, a bonfire) so that the light reading is taken from here. When you take the shot, the main subject will be underexposed, i.e. too dark, but this will create the silhouette effect.

6 Transferring Photos

Once digital photos have been captured on a camera it is important to get them onto a computer so that they can be printed or edited. This chapter covers the ways to do this for both Windows and Macs.

Using a Docking Station

Once you have taken photos on your camera the next step is to transfer them onto your computer. There are a number of ways of doing this, and perhaps the best option is to use a docking station as this does not involve removing the camera's memory card or connecting the camera each time you want to download images. A docking station is a device that connects to the computer; the camera is placed in the docking station to download the photos. To download photos using a docking station:

Beware

Not all digital cameras come with docking stations: Kodak has the largest range of cameras that use them.

1 Place the camera in the docking station

Don't forget

Docking stations also charge the camera's batteries, but only after the downloading process has been completed.

2 Attach the supplied cable to the docking station

3 Connect the docking station to the computer with the supplied USB cable

Don't forget

Docking stations can be left connected to the computer permanently once you have installed them.

4 The software should recognize the docking station and the downloading process will begin

Transfer

Found Z650 Zoom Digital Camera

Select or type in new destination album: World Tour

☐ Remove pictures from original device (if supported)

☐ Next time perform a One-Touch Transfer

Transfer All   Select and Transfer...   Cancel   More Options...   Help

Don't forget

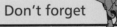

The software that is provided with the docking station is used to download photos from the camera and it can also be used to edit, organize, print and share the photos.

5 Once the photos have been downloaded they will be available via the software that is provided with the docking station

From Camera to Computer

Another option for downloading photos is to connect your camera directly to your computer. This is done with a cable that should be supplied with the camera.

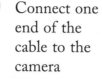 Connect one end of the cable to the camera

Connect the other end of the cable to the computer. This is usually done with a USB (Universal Serial Bus) connection

Turn on the camera

Depending on your computer's operating system, it should recognize the type of camera and prepare to download the photos

Using a Memory Card Reader

You can also download photos from a camera to a computer by using a memory card reader, which is a device that can be connected to the computer. The camera's memory card can be inserted into the card reader. Many card readers will work with all of the different types of memory card on the market. To use a memory card reader:

1 Connect the memory card reader to your computer using the cable that should be supplied with the card reader

2 Remove the memory card from the camera

3 Insert the memory card into the card reader

4 The card reader will show up as a separate drive on your computer:

Devices with Removable Storage (7)

Floppy Disk Drive (A:)

CD Drive (E:)

DVD Drive (F:) 080519_1722
0 bytes free of 323 MB

Card Reader (H:)

Don't forget

Card readers that can accommodate a variety of memory cards are known as multi card readers. Look for this type of card reader, as they are more versatile.

Don't forget

When a memory card is inserted into a card reader, the computer will usually recognize this and begin the downloading process.

Downloading with Windows

Once you have connected your camera or card reader to the computer you can download photos onto the computer. If you are using the Windows operating system this can be done with the AutoPlay function:

1 Connect your camera, or a card reader, to your computer

2 The AutoPlay window will be activated

3 Click on the Import Pictures Using Windows option

4 Enter a tag for the photos, if required

5   Click on the Import button   Import

6   The photos are downloaded from your camera or card reader

Importing Pictures and Videos

NIKON D70 (F:)

Importing item 53 of 55

☐ Erase after importing

Cancel

7   The photos can be viewed in the appropriate folder in the Pictures folder on your computer

◄ Nick ► Pictures ► Snow

8   Click on the folder name to access the photos within it, i.e. the ones that have just been downloaded

Hot tip

It is a good idea to create a new folder for each new batch of photos downloaded.

Downloading in Photo Editors

If you do not want to use the Windows operating system to download your photos you can use a photo editing program, such as Photoshop Elements. This has the advantage of saving the photos within the photo editing program's system, which can make it easier to organize your photos at a later date. To download photos with Photoshop Elements:

1 If Photoshop Elements is installed on your computer and a camera or a card reader is connected to the computer, the program recognizes this, launches automatically and opens the Downloader window

2 Click in the Get Photos From box and select the device from which you want to download photos

3 Click on the Browse button to select a destination on your hard drive where you want the photos to be saved

...cont'd

4 Click the Get Photos button

5 The photos are downloaded from the device

	Copying - 3% Completed	

From: **F:\<NIKON D70>**

To: C:\Users\Nick\Pictures\Nick_pics\2008 11 23

3%

File 3 of 55: Copying File...

DSC_0125.JPG

Minimize | Stop

6 The photos are then copied into the Photoshop Elements Organizer area

7 The downloaded photos are displayed on their own in the program's Organizer section

8 Click on the Show All button to view all of the photos that have been downloaded with the program

Viewing Photos

Once photos have been downloaded onto your computer (using Windows) they can be viewed in a number of ways:

1 To begin viewing photos, click the Start button

2 Click on the Pictures option

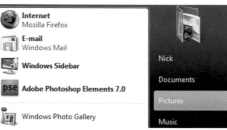

3 In the Pictures window all of the folders containing photos are displayed.

4 Double-click on a folder to open it and view its contents

5 From within a photo folder, click on the Views button

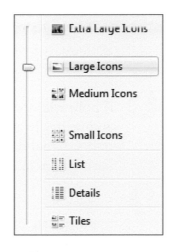

6 Select one of the options for viewing your photos

7 The options in Step 6 determine the size at which photos are displayed within their folder

Snow 053

Don't forget

The photos folder toolbar appears at the top of folders containing photos.

8 The photos folder toolbar also has options for displaying photos in other programs, as slideshows and also for printing, emailing, sharing and burning to CD or DVD

▼ Preview ▼ Slide Show Print E-mail Share Burn

Downloading with a Mac

If you use an Apple Mac computer the downloading process is taken over by the computer, using a program called iPhoto that comes already installed on all new Macs. To download photos with a Mac:

Don't forget

iPhoto is a photo editing program. It can be used as the default program for downloading photos on a Mac.

1 Connect the camera or card reader to the computer

2 iPhoto will open automatically and recognize that a digital device has been connected

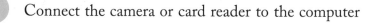

3 Enter a name for the batch of photos that you want to download and give them a description

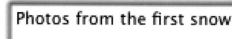

Event Name: | Winter

Description: | Photos from the first snow

4 Select the photos you want to download and click

Import Selected   Import All...

on the Import Selected button. Otherwise, click on the Import All button

5 Under the Library heading, click on the Photos button to see all of the photos that have been downloaded into iPhoto

LIBRARY
Events
Photos

6 Under the Recent heading, click on the Last Import button to see the photos that you have just downloaded

7 The photos are displayed in the main iPhoto window

8 Drag this slider to change the size at which the photos are displayed

9 Click on this button to view the images in the Library window as a slideshow

10 Select an image and click on this button to view it at full screen size

Editing on a Mac

iPhoto is a powerful program for organizing photos on a Mac and it can also be used to perform a number of photo editing tasks. To do this:

98

1 Click on a photo that you want to edit

2 Click on the Edit button

3 The photo is displayed within the Editing environment

4 Click on these buttons to rotate the orientation of a photo, crop out any unwanted background or straighten an image that is misaligned (such as one that has been scanned)

5 Click on the Enhance button to automatically edit all of the color elements in the photo

6 Click on the Adjust button to access the window for editing specific elements within the photo

Don't forget

Make small editing changes at a time and view the results as you are going along. This will ensure that the changes are not too extreme or drastic.

7 The Adjust window has sliders for altering various color elements within the photo

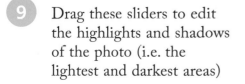

8 Drag these sliders to edit the exposure and contrast of the photo

9 Drag these sliders to edit the highlights and shadows of the photo (i.e. the lightest and darkest areas)

99

...cont'd

10 Drag these sliders to edit the amount and type of color in the photo

11 Drag these sliders to make the photo crisper (Sharpness) and remove any unwanted, random colored pixels (Reduce Noise)

12 Click on the Effects button to access the window for different color or artistic effects

Effects

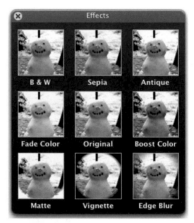

Don't forget

If you want to do more advanced editing on the Mac, look at the Aperture program, or a version of Photoshop.

13 Editing changes appear in the photo as they are being made

14 Click on the Done button to apply the editing changes i.e. save them

Creating a Digital Shoebox

When all photos came in printed format it was easy to collect vast numbers of photos that were hardly ever looked at. Drawers and shoeboxes were filled with photos and packed away in cupboards and attics. With the digital age the need for physically storing photos has been greatly reduced. However, our computers have now become the equivalent of the old-fashioned shoebox and it is easy to get hundreds, or thousands, of photos scattered around different locations on your computer. To try and overcome this, and give some order to your digital shoebox, it is worth creating a file structure into which your photos can be saved when they are downloaded. To do this:

1 Click the Start button

2 Select the Pictures button

3 Within the Pictures folder, click on the Organize button

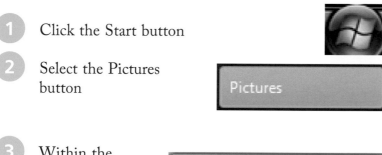

4 Click the New Folder button

New Folder

5 Give the folder a top-level name for a collection of photos, such as Vacations

Vacations

...cont'd

6 Double-click on the new folder to open it. At this point it will be empty

7 Repeat Steps 4 and 5 to create subfolders of the top-level one. These could be for specific years or locations

Name	Date taken	Tags

Africa   Europe

Don't forget

New folders and subfolders can be added to a file structure at any time.

8 Keep creating subfolders until you have created a suitable file structure

USA

9 Click on the Folders button to view the complete file structure

Folders

Folders

Snow

◢ Vacations

    Africa

    Europe

    USA

7 Examining Photos

This chapter shows how digital photographs are created and how to resize them to suit the way you want to use them.

Dissecting a Digital Photo

Since digital photographs are made up of a collection of colored building blocks (pixels), there is a great deal of flexibility when it comes to viewing and editing them. Using a photo editing program, you can edit each individual pixel – i.e. change its color – as well as changing large areas of a photograph. By looking at a digital photograph in a photo editing program, you can understand more about how they are created. To do this, with Photoshop Elements:

Don't forget

For more information about using Photoshop Elements to work with digital photos, see Chapter Eight.

1 Open an image in a photo editing program. By default the whole image will be visible

Don't forget

The most common file format for digital photographs is JPEG, which stands for Joint Photograph Experts Group. This is the format in which most digital cameras capture photographs.

2 At the top of the editing window are details of the file name and the file format (in this case it is a JPEG, denoted by the .jpg extension)

3 The size at which the image is being viewed is displayed next to the file name

4 By increasing the magnification of the image, individual areas can be seen more closely

5 By increasing the magnification to its full value, individual pixels can be viewed

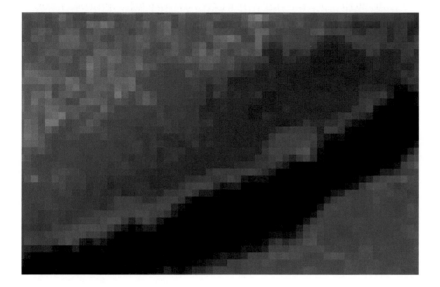

Don't forget

Photo editing (including viewing images at different sizes) is looked at in more detail in Chapter Eight.

105

6 Photo editing can be used to edit individual pixels in a digital photo

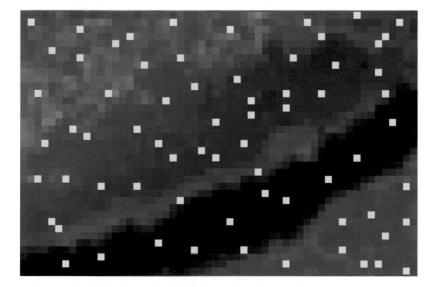

The Resolution Riddle

In the world of digital photography you will sooner or later (probably sooner) come across the concept of resolution. While this term refers to a number of different aspects of digital photography, the most important one relates to the size of images in terms of pixels (the colored electronic building blocks that make up digital images).

Photo resolution

When looking at a digital camera you will be quoted a headline figure giving the number of pixels it can capture for each photograph. This can either be stated as an overall headline figure, e.g. 8 million pixels (or 8 megapixels), or as the dimensions of an image (e.g. 1800 pixels x 1200 pixels).

Most digital cameras can capture images at various different resolution settings (with different numbers of pixels). A camera's manual will tell you the number of pixels at each setting. This is sometimes referred to as the image size or image dimensions.

The importance of pixels and resolution is that they determine the size at which images can be displayed on a computer monitor and printed to a high quality.

Printed images

Most people want to print at least some of their digital photographs and, as a general rule, for printed images you want as many pixels as possible.

For printed images a setting of 300 pixels per inch (ppi) is used for optimum quality. This means that each linear inch of the printed image will contain 300 pixels. To work out the size of the final printed image that can be printed at high quality, divide the pixel dimensions of the image by 300. So an image with a resolution of 1800 x 1200 would be printable at high quality at 6 inches x 4 inches. If the resolution of the image were lower, i.e. it had fewer pixels, it could still be printed at the same size but the result would be of inferior quality as there would be fewer pixels in each inch of the image.

Beware

The various elements connected with resolution in digital photography can be confusing so it is worth spending a bit of time coming to terms with each one.

106

The following table illustrates the resolution, in terms of number of pixels, required for various sizes of prints (presuming that they are printed at 300 ppi).

Overall pixels	Dimensions (pixels)	Print size (inches at 300 ppi)
8 million	3264 x 2448	11 x 8 (approx.)
5 million	2592 x 1944	8 x 6 (approx.)
3 million	2048 x 1536	7 x 5 (approx.)
1 million	1280 x 960	4 x 3 (approx.)

When capturing images that you know will be printed, do so with the largest number of pixels possible, i.e. at the highest image size setting on your camera.

Web images

Images on the Web are traditionally displayed at about 72 ppi as this is the resolution of standard computer monitors. This means that in a linear inch of the screen 72 pixels of the digital photo arc displaycd. Because of this, photos for the Web can be captured at a considerably smaller size, i.e. fewer pixels, than ones that are going to be printed.

Recap

- For photos for printing, use the highest resolution setting on your camera, i.e. the most pixels

- For photos for the Web, use a lower resolution setting

- If in doubt, use the highest resolution setting (photos can be made smaller later with photo editing programs)

- To work out the size of printed photos, divide the pixel dimensions (height and width) of a photo by 300

- To work out the size of online photos, divide the pixel dimensions (height and width) of a photo by 72

Don't forget

When looking at digital cameras remember that the headline figure that is quoted by manufacturers or retailers (e.g. 5 megapixels) is the number of pixels captured at the camera's highest reolution setting.

Making Photos Smaller

Since digital photographs are made up of individual pixels it is possible to reduce the size of the photos by removing pixels from the original. This has to be done with a photo editing program on a computer. One of the most common reasons for making images smaller is so that they can be viewed at their actual size on a computer without having to scroll around the screen to see the whole photo. To make a photo smaller, using Photoshop Elements:

Hot tip

Whenever you are editing digital photos, always make a copy first, using the Save As command within your photo editing program. This can then be used for editing, leaving the master copy intact.

1 Open a photo in your chosen photo editing program and view it at its actual size, i.e. 100% magnification (depending on the size of the image this may make it larger than the monitor on which it is being viewed, in which case you will only see part of it)

2 Access the Image Size window within the photo editing program. This is usually done from the program's Menu bar by selecting an option similar to Image>Resize>Image Size

3 The Image Size window contains all of the necessary functions for changing the size of the photo

4 Make sure that the Resample Image and the Constrain Proportions boxes are both checked

5 The current dimensions (in pixels) of the photo are shown in the Pixel Dimensions section of the Image Size window

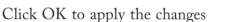

6 Enter a lower number in the Width or Height box to make the photo smaller

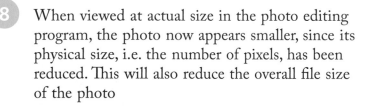

7 Click OK to apply the changes

8 When viewed at actual size in the photo editing program, the photo now appears smaller, since its physical size, i.e. the number of pixels, has been reduced. This will also reduce the overall file size of the photo

Don't forget

The process of making digital photos smaller or larger is know as resampling. Making photos smaller is known as resampling down and making photos larger is known as resampling up.

Hot tip

The link symbol connecting the Width and Height boxes appears when the Constrain Proportions box is checked.

Making Photos Larger

The process for making digital photos larger is similar to that for making them smaller, except that pixels are added rather than removed. The photo editing program adds pixels to the photo through a process of complex digital guesswork known as interpolation. This involves looking at the existing pixels in the photo and then working out the best possible color for new pixels that are added next to the existing ones. Although this sounds a bit hit and miss, it is surprisingly accurate and it can be hard to notice the difference afterwards. The most common use for making photos larger is so that they can be printed at a higher quality and/or larger size. To make a photo larger:

Beware

Making digital photos larger by adding more pixels does result in a slight deterioration in quality, but this is not always noticeable.

1 Open a photo in your chosen photo editing program

2 Access the Image Size window

3 Make sure that the Resample Image and Constrain Proportions boxes are checked

☑ Constrain Proportions

☑ Resample Image: Bicubic

4 The current dimensions (in pixels) of the photo are shown in the Pixel Dimensions section of the Image Size window

Pixel Dimensions: 800.6K

Width: 640 pixels

Height: 427 pixels

5 Enter a higher number in the Width or Height box to make the photo larger

Pixel Dimensions: 2.75M (was 800.6K)

Width: 1200 pixels

Height: 801 pixels

6 Click OK to apply the changes

OK

Preparing for Printing

If you want to get photos printed by someone else, such as a photographic retail store or an online service, make sure that the photos are captured at the camera's highest available image size, i.e. the one with the most pixels.

If you want to print photos yourself on a home printer it is still important to capture the photos at the highest image size. Once this has been done, you can then use a photo editing program to specify the size and quality at which you want the photos to be printed. To do this:

① Open a photo in your photo editing program and access the Image Size window within the photo editing program. This is usually done from the program's Menu bar by selecting an option similar to Image>Resize>Image Size

② The number of pixels in the photo is shown at the top of the Image Size window

Pixel Dimensions: 17.2M

Width: 3000 pixels

Height: 2008 pixels

③ To retain the current number of pixels, make sure the Resample Image box is not checked

Resample Image:

④ The size of the printed photo is determined by the figure in the Resolution box in the Document Size section. In this example this results in a printed image of 10 x 6.7 inches, i.e. 3000 divided by 300 and 2008 divided by 300

Document Size:

Width: 10 inches

Height: 6.693 inches

Resolution: 300 pixels/inch

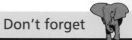
If a checkbox is not checked then it is empty. If it is checked, a colored tick will appear in the box.

...cont'd

5 If you want
to print
the photo
at a larger
size, enter
the relevant
figures in
the Width and Height boxes. In the example, the
Width was set to 12 inches, giving a proportional
size of 7.03 inches for the Height. This results in
a print resolution of 250 pixels per inch, i.e. 3000
divided by 12 and 2008 divided by 8.03

Document Size:		
Width: 12	inches	▼
Height: 8.032	inches	▼
Resolution: 250	pixels/inch	▼

6 If you want to increase
the number of pixels in a
photo (in order to retain
the document size settings)
check the Resample
Image box

✔ Resample Image:

7 The print
resolution
of the photo
can now be
increased
without
changing the
Width and
Height sizes

Document Size:		
Width: 12	inches	▼
Height: 8.032	inches	▼
Resolution: 300	pixels/inch	▼

8 To accommodate
the increase in
resolution, the
number of pixels in
the photo has been
increased by the
photo editing software

Pixel Dimensions: 24.8M (was 17.2M)

Width: 3600	pixels	▼
Height: 2410	pixels	▼

Preparing for the Web

If digital photos are going to be used online, i.e. displayed on a Web page, it is important that the image is not too large, in terms of both file size and pixel dimensions. This is because a large file will take longer to download on a Web page and also because a large photo may take up too much space on the monitor. Most photo editing programs have an option for saving photos for the Web:

1️⃣ Select File>Save For Web from the Menu bar

2️⃣ The Save For Web window offers several options for saving the photo and reducing its file size and number of pixels

3️⃣ The left-hand panel displays the photo and its current settings. The right-hand panel shows details of the photo once the changes have been made

Don't forget

When preparing images for the Web, divide the number of pixels in the Height and Width of the image by 72 to work out the approximate size (in inches) at which it will be viewed on a Web page.

113

…cont'd

4 The Save For Web window has options for the way the photo is saved. These include the file format and the quality. A reduction in the Quality value results in the size of the file being reduced but it does not always lead to a noticeable reduction in image quality

 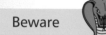
Preset: Custom
JPEG
High   Quality: 60
☐ Progressive
☑ ICC Profile   Matte:

5 In the Image Size section of the Save For Web window, the physical size of the photo can be changed by entering new figures in the Width and Height boxes. This can be done to ensure that a photo is displayed at a smaller size on the Web

Image Size
Original Size
Width: 3000 pixels
Height: 2008 pixels

New Size
Width: 3000 pixels
Height: 2008 pixels
Percent: 100
☑ Constrain Proportions
Apply

6 Click OK to apply any editing changes that have been made

OK

8 Editing Photos

Digital photo editing on a computer is a great way to improve elements of photos and also have some fun with them. This chapter offers advice about choosing a program and also shows some common, and easy to learn, photo editing techniques.

Picking an Editing Program

Photo editing programs are used on computers to manipulate digital photos. There are a wide variety available and they vary considerably in terms of functions and price. For the examples in this book, Photoshop Elements is used. This is an excellent program in terms of functions, value for money and ease of use and fulfils all of the criteria for a general-use photo editing program. The main functions of Photoshop Elements are:

Editing
Elements provides powerful editing functions, within a clear interface that includes a number of Help options:

Don't forget

For more information about Photoshop Elements, have a look at "Photoshop Elements 7 In Easy Steps" in this series.

The editing functions within Photoshop Elements are presented in a Tools panel that contains the selection tools, crop tool, red-eye removal tool, text tool, coloring tools and cloning tools. There is also a Menu bar that can be used to access common commands and a Toolbar for functions such as opening new files, printing, and accessing other areas of the program such as the Organizer section, the Create section and the Share section.

…cont'd

Organizing

A whole area is given over to organizing photos so that they can be easily found and sorted:

Hot tip

When Photoshop Elements is first opened, there are options for accessing the different parts of the program.

Creating

As well as editing and organizing, Elements also has several options for using digital photos, including creating slide shows and creative emails, and even publishing them on your own Web page:

Viewing Photos

The first thing that most people want to do with a photo editing program is to look at their photos. Once photos have been opened within a photo editing program, they can then be viewed at different magnifications.

Opening photos

The procedure for opening photos with a photo editing program is virtually the same, regardless of the program. To do this:

 Select File>Open from the Menu bar

 Browse to the photos that are on your computer and click on one to select it

 Click Open to open the selected photo in the photo editing program

 The photo is opened within the photo editing program, ready for editing

Magnifying images

By default, photos are opened within a photo editing program so that you can see all of them. However, there will be occasions when you will want to zoom in on a particular part of a photo, for editing purposes. There are various ways in which this can be done, but one of the best is by using the Zoom tool. To do this:

1 Open an image

2 Click on the Zoom tool in the Tools panel

3 Position the Zoom tool over part of an image. If a plus sign is showing this will zoom in on the photo

4 Click on part of the photo to zoom in on it

5 Press Alt and click on the photo to change the function to zoom out, which is denoted by a minus sign in the Zoom tool

Don't forget

When carrying out certain editing functions, such as selecting areas, it can be beneficial to zoom in on the photo to edit parts of it as accurately as possible.

Selecting Areas

One of the most important aspects of image editing is the ability to select areas within an image. This can be used in a number of different ways:

- Selecting an object to apply an editing technique to it (such as changing the brightness or contrast) without affecting the rest of the image

- Selecting a particular color in an image

- Selecting an area to apply a special effect to it

- Selecting an area to remove it

There are usually three options in photo editing programs for selecting areas:

Lasso tool

120

1   Open an image

2   Select the Lasso tool

3   Make a freehand selection by clicking and dragging around an object

Polygonal Lasso tool

 Select the Polygonal Lasso tool

2 Make a
selection
by clicking
on specific
points
around
an object
and then
dragging to
the
next point

Magnetic Lasso tool

1 Select the Magnetic Lasso tool

2 Click once on an image to create
the first anchor point

3 Make a
selection by
dragging
continuously
around an
object. The
selection
line snaps to
the closest
strongest edge,
i.e. the one

with the most contrast. Fastening points are added as
the selection is made

Beware

If there is not enough
contrast between
elements when using
the Magnetic Lasso
tool, the selection may
jump erratically.

Brightening Dull Photos

When taking digital photos, sometimes the end result is either slightly too dark or too light. This can be because of the lighting conditions at the time or because of the way that the camera works. Either way, this is not a serious problem because the lighting can be improved within a photo editing program. To do this:

Hot tip

It is usually more effective to lighten dark photos than to darken light ones.

 Open a photo that looks either too dark or too light

 Access the Brightness/Contrast command by selecting Enhance>Adjust Lighting>Brightness/Contrast from the Menu bar

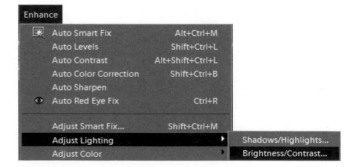

3 Drag the sliders for Brightness and Contrast to lighten or darken the image

4 Click the OK button

OK

5 The selected options will be applied to the photo

Hot tip

Other options for lightening photos are to use the Levels command (Enhance>Adjust Lighting>Levels from the Menu bar) or the Shadows and Highlights command (Enhance>Adjust Lighting>Shadows/Highlights from the Menu bar).

123

6 Save the photo to keep the changes, by selecting File>Save from the Menu bar

Making Photos Crisper

One result of taking photos with digital technology is that they are sometimes not as crisp as film photographs and can appear slightly "soft". This is not always apparent with the naked eye but it can be seen in photo editing programs if the photo is magnified. Photo editing programs can also be used to make the image appear crisper, a process known as sharpening. To do this:

Hot tip

Most digital cameras have a facility for sharpening photos when they are taken. This can be accessed from the camera's menu system.

Don't forget

Other options for sharpening are Sharpen, Sharpen Edges and Sharpen More. These do not require any settings to be chosen so they do not have a dialog box.

1 Open a photo. Initially, it may not look as if it needs to be made crisper

2 Access the Sharpen commands by selecting Filter>Sharpen from the Menu bar

3 Select the Unsharp Mask option

4 The Unsharp Mask window gives options for making the photo crisper

Unsharp Mask

OK

Cancel

✓ Preview

— 100% +

Amount: 100 %

Radius: 1.0 pixels

Threshold: 0 levels

5 Drag the Amount slider to change the level of sharpening

6 The Preview box shows how the level of sharpening affects the photo

7 Click OK

OK

8 The photo will now look crisper

Beware

If too much sharpening is applied it can make the photo look unnatural and too jaggy. Therefore, apply sharpening in small amounts and reapply the technique if required.

Using the Best Parts

With most digital photos there are areas that do not add anything to the photo and in some cases they detract from it. This could be an unwanted background behind a photo of grandchildren or a large area of unwanted sky behind a famous landmark. A technique known as cropping can be used to remove unwanted areas of a photo, leaving just the best parts. To do this:

1 Open a photo that has an area of unwanted background

2 The Crop tool is located within the Tools panel

3 Click on the Crop tool in the Tools panel

4 Drag around the part of the photo that you want to keep

Hot tip

Photoshop Elements has a function for constraining the size of the cropped area to certain proportions. This is useful if you want to print the photo at a specific size, e.g. 7 x 5 inches.

127

5 Click the tick to apply the cropping changes

6 The cropped part is now the whole photo

Getting Artistic

Photo editing programs have a variety of special effects that can be added to photos. These can be used to create an artistic effect or to make a surreal image from the photo. Effects can be accessed from the Filter menu on the Menu bar or from the Styles and Effects panel. To add artistic effects:

128

 Open a photo to which you want to add effects

 Access the Styles and Effects panel by selecting Window>Styles and Effects from the Menu bar

 Double-click a style or effect to apply it to the currently open image

4 Some Styles and Effects have additional windows in which the properties for the style or effect can be set

5 The selected style or effect is applied to the image

Adding Messages

Adding messages to digital photos is a great way to personalize photos and give them an extra dimension. This is done by writing on a photo with the Text tool. To do this:

Hot tip

Adding messages is an excellent way to create your own digital postcards.

1 Open a photo to which you want to add a message

Beware

Use a text color that has a good contrast with the background onto which it is going to be placed.

2 Click here to select the Text tool on the Tools panel

3 Click here to select the font

Verdana

4 Click here to select the size

60 pt

5 Click here to select the color

6 Click on the photo at the point where you want to start typing

7 Type the message

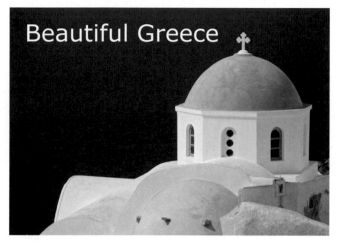

Make sure that the text is large enough so that it can be read easily on the photo.

8 To move the message, select the Move tool on the Tools panel

9 Click on the text box and drag it to move the message around the photo

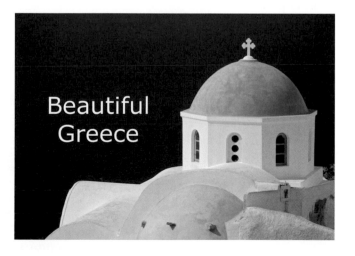

Airbrushing Photos

One of the most effective and striking editing techniques for digital photos is airbrushing. This involves removing or altering part of the original photo. This could be to remove blemishes in the photo, or to remove large elements such as people or buildings. Airbrushing is achieved with the Clone tool, which is used to copy one part of the photo over another. To airbrush a photo using the Clone tool:

Hot tip

Airbrushing can be used to remove spots or wrinkles from faces and also for fun techniques such as restyling someone's hair.

1 Open a photo that contains an item you want to remove

2 Click on the Clone tool on the Tools panel (this is sometimes also known as the Stamp tool)

3 Hold down Alt and click on the part of the photo that you want to use to cover the area to be removed. This serves to load the Clone tool

④ Move the cursor over the part of the photo that you want to airbrush out

⑤ Click and drag over the required element. The area selected in Step 3 is now copied onto the area over which the cursor passes

Hot tip

Perform the cloning in small steps and release the mouse regularly. This will enable you to undo each step if it has gone wrong, without having to undo the whole process, which would be the only option if you had not released the mouse button.

⑥ Try cloning from different areas to create a smooth background for the cloned area

Adding Family Members

When capturing photos of family groups it is inevitable that one person (or more) is not there at the time. Instead of leaving them out of the final photo, it is possible to use a photo editing program to add them to the original photo. To do this:

1 Open a photo of the missing person

Selections can also be made using the Magnetic Lasso tool and the Polygonal Lasso tool.

2 Click on the Lasso tool in the Tools panel

3 Click and drag around the missing person to make a selection. This does not have to be too accurate

4 Select Edit>Copy from the Menu bar

5 Open the photo of the family group

6 Select Edit>Paste from the Menu bar

7 The copied selection is pasted into the group photo

Don't forget

Don't worry if the pasted selection looks too large as it can easily be resized (see next page).

...cont'd

8 Zoom in on the pasted selection and click on the Eraser tool in the Tools panel

9 Click and drag to remove any unwanted parts of the selection

10 Click on the Move tool

11 Hold down the Shift key and drag on one of the corner markers around the selection. This will enable you to resize it proportionally

12 Use the Move tool to position the missing person within the complete group

13 General editing techniques can then be applied to the photo, such as editing the overall color

Organizing Photos

In addition to being able to edit photos, most photo editing programs have a facility for organizing photos so that you can find them quickly. In Photoshop Elements this is done within the Organizer section of the program. To use this:

1 Access the Organizer button

2 Click on the Display button and select the Date View option

Undo Redo	Display ▾
Thumbnail View	Ctrl+Alt+1
Import Batch	Ctrl+Alt+2
Folder Location	Ctrl+Alt+3
Date View	Ctrl+Alt+D

Don't forget

Digital photo collections can grow very quickly and you will soon realize the value of using an organizing program.

3 Select a date to view the photos that were downloaded then

● **MARCH 2009** ●

Sun	Mon	Tue	Wed	Thu	Fri	Sat
1	2	3	4	5	6	7
8	9	10	11	12	13	14
15	16	17	18	19	20	21

4 Double-click on a date to view the relevant photos in the Photo Browser

Creating Albums

Within the Organizer, albums can be created so that they can be found quickly. To do this:

1 Click on the Albums tab within the Photo Browser

2 Click on the green plus sign and click on the New Album button

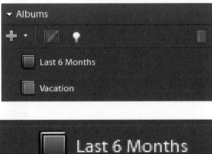

3 Enter a name for the new album

4 Drag photos into the new album

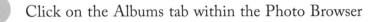

5 Click here to view all of the items within an album

...cont'd

Adding keywords

Keywords can also be added to photos, to help with finding them later. To do this:

1 Click on the Keyword Tags section

2 Click on green plus sign and click on the New Keyword Tag button

3 Create a new keyword tag

4 Drag the keyword tag onto a photo, or group of photos

5 Click here next to the relevant keyword

6 The photos in the collection will be displayed

9 Using Photos and Email

Email is a quick way to share your photos with family and friends.

Getting the Right Size

Email is one of the most popular uses for digital photos and it is easy to see why:

- It is quick. Photos of family, friends or newborn grandchildren can be distributed around the globe in a matter of minutes from the time they are taken

- It is cheap. Once you have an Internet connection there is no additional cost in sending a photo by email

- It is inclusive. Large numbers of people can be sent the same photos, at the same time

Before looking at the details of sending and receiving photos by email, it is useful to look at the issue of file size. When you are emailing digital photos there are two important considerations:

- Will the photos be viewed in an online environment, i.e. on a computer monitor?

- Will the photos be printed?

This is important because photos for use online can be considerably smaller, in terms of physical size and of file size, than those for printing. There are three ways to make your photos the correct size for the use to which they will be put:

- Set the size when capturing the photo. As shown in Chapter 2, page 30, the picture size can be specified within the camera's menu system. If you know your photo is going to be viewed online you can set the size to a lower setting, e.g. 2 megapixels. Conversely, if you know the photo will be printed out, then select the highest value for the picture size, e.g. 6 megapixels. The larger the picture size the greater the overall file size

- Let your software set the size automatically (see Chapter Seven, page 113 for details) when preparing photos for the Web or email

- Set the size manually with software (see Chapter Seven, pages 108–110 for details)

Sending Photos by Email

Once you have downloaded your photos and got them ready for sending to family and friends you can then start the process of attaching them to an email. There are two ways in which this can be done:

- Directly from a photo editing program

- By attaching the photo to an email in an email program, such as Mail or Outlook Express

Sending with a photo editing program

All photo editing programs differ slightly in how they operate, but the process is generally like this:

- You open up a photo in the photo editing program

- Select the Email Photo option

- Select various options for adding text and, in some cases, artistic formatting to the photo

- Send the email with the photo included

To send a photo by email using Photoshop Elements:

Don't forget

Sending a photo with a photo editing program gives you more scope for creating an artistic design and appearance.

143

 1 Access the Organizer area and select a photo

2 Click on the Share button

...cont'd

3 In the E-mail window, select your email program and click on the Continue button

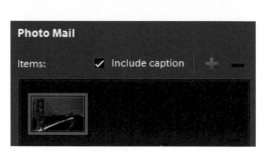

4 The selected image is displayed within the Photo Mail section

5 Click on the Next button

6 Enter the message for the email. This will appear in the body of the email

7 Enter an email address for the recipient or select one from your address book

8 Select the formatting options for the email. This gives the photo email a more designed look

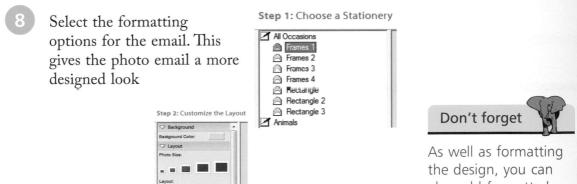

Step 1: Choose a Stationery

- All Occasions
  - Frames 1
  - Frames 2
  - Frames 3
  - Frames 4
  - Rectangle
  - Rectangle 2
  - Rectangle 3
- Animals

Step 2: Customize the Layout

Don't forget

As well as formatting the design, you can also add formatted text to the photo email message.

9 Click on the Next button to move to the next step of the process

Next

10 Your email program will open automatically, with the formatted photo email already prepared. Click Send to send the email

...cont'd

Sending with an email program

1 Open your email program and click on the Create Mail button to create a new, blank email

2 The email opens but with no content

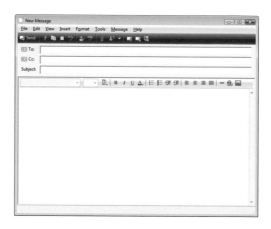

3 Enter an email address for the recipient

4 Enter a subject for the email in the Subject box

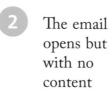

5 Enter text for the email

6 Click on this button to attach a photo

7 Browse your hard drive to the location of the photo that you want to attach

8 Select the photo you want and click on the Open button

9 Details of the photo (including its file size) appear in the Attach box that is now included in the header of the email

10 Click Send to send the email in the normal way

⊞ To:	nickvandome@mac.com <nickvandome@mac.com>;
⊞ Cc:	
Subject:	Vacation
Attach:	🖼 boston5.jpg (58.6 KB) 🖼 boston6.jpg (85.2 KB)

🖳 Send

Viewing Photos from Email

Once you have received a photo in an email there are two ways in which it can be viewed, without saving it first:

Viewing within an email

Depending on the type of email program, the photo can be viewed directly within the body of the email:

1 Open the email

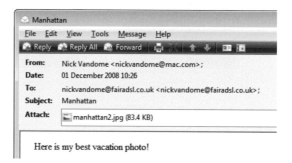

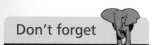
2 If the photo is not visible, scroll down the window until the photo comes into view

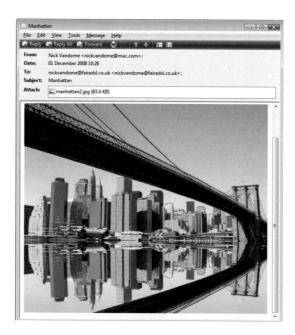

Opening from an email

It is possible to open a photo directly from an email:

1 Double-click on the photo icon in the Attach box

Attach: manhattan2.jpg (83.4 KB)

2 The photo will be opened in your default photo editing program. At this point the photo will not be saved to your computer

Saving Photos from Email

When you receive a photo in an email you will probably want to save it to your hard drive, or an external device, so that you can view the photo at any time and manipulate it if required. There are two ways to do this:

From the Menu bar
Photo attachments can also be saved by using commands from the Menu bar. To do this:

 Open the email with the photo attachment

 Select File>Save Attachments from the Menu bar

File	Edit	View	Tools
New			
Save As...			
Save Attachments...			

 The Save Attachments dialog window displays the attachment that will be saved. Click the Save button

Save Attachments

Attachments To Be Saved:

manhattan2.jpg (83.4 KB)   Save

 Click the Browse button to navigate to a location on your hard drive where you want to save the attachment

Save To
C:\Users\Nick\Documents\DP Seniors v2   Browse...

 Click the Save button to save the photo attachment to the destination selected in Step 4

Save Attachment As
« Documents › DP Seniors v2 ›   Search
File name: manhattan2
Save as type: Attachment (*.*)
Browse Folders   Save   Cancel

10 Sharing on the Web

Online sharing services are a way to share photos on the Web with chosen family and friends.

How to Share Photos

Online photo sharing services now proliferate on the Web and it is easy to see why: they offer a wide range of services for sharing and printing photos; they are secure and good value; and they can be accessed directly from your own computer. Once you have joined a photo sharing site, you can also access it from any computer that is connected to the Internet.

Using a photo sharing site is just a question of accessing a website. There are dozens of different photo sharing sites but the processes for using them are virtually identical:

- Once you have found a site that you want to use, you have to register. However, this is free and usually only involves giving your name, an email address and a password

- Once you are registered you can start using the site. The first step is to create individual albums into which you can save your photos. Different albums can be created for a variety of topics

- After an album has been created it can be shared with other people. This is done by sending them an email inviting them to view your photos. Only people you have invited can view your online photo albums. It is usually free to share photos on an online site; if you are ever asked for a fee just for sharing photos, look for another site

- Photos in albums can also be used for online printing. Almost all online sharing services also have a facility for producing prints from your photos and sending them to you. This is one of the ways in which the sites make their money and they always try to promote this side of their service

- Online sharing sites also have a wide range of other merchandise onto which you can put your photos. This includes cards, calendars, jigsaws, mugs, T-shirts and even bags and cushions

Getting Registered

Unlike a lot of commercial online services, registering for an online sharing service is quick and easy and is not something that anyone should worry about. Registration is free and there is no obligation to spend any money, unless you want to buy some of the site's products. Remember, the photo sharing part of the site should be free. For all photo sharing sites the registration process is virtually the same:

1. Access the site and click on the Register or Register Now button (on some sites the registration boxes are directly on the homepage)

2. Enter your name, email address and password

3. Click the Create Account button to complete registration

4. Once you have registered you will be taken to your own secure homepage within the site. This is where you can start creating albums and sharing photos

One Step to Create an Account

* **First Name:**
Nick

* **Email Address:**
nickvandome@mac.com

* **Create Password:** 6 character min.
•••••••

* **Re-type Password:**
•••••••

☐ **Add Your Camera Phone**
Enter your mobile phone number to be able to upload your camera phone pictures to the Gallery.

* ☑ I agree to use **Kodak** Gallery in accordance with the Terms of Service.

☐ Yes! Send me special offers and news from the KODAK Gallery Team. See examples.

Create Account

View & Edit Photos

My Albums
Choose an album to view

Create
New Album

153

Hot tip

When registering for an online sharing service, give them an online email address (such as Hotmail) if you have one. This is because they will send you a lot of marketing email in an effort to persuade you to use other services.

Assessing Online Services

There are dozens of online sharing services on the Web and which one you choose may just be down to personal taste and the first impression when you look at the homepage. However, some areas to look at include:

- The range of services offered

- Any restrictions on the number of photos you can store and share

- The price for online prints and merchandise

A few online sharing service to consider are:

Shutterfly at www.shutterfly.com

Hot tip

More online sites can be found by entering "online sharing" into a search engine such as Google.

154

Don't forget

UK sites include:

PhotoBox at
www.photobox.co.uk

Snapfish at
www.snapfish.co.uk

Kodak at
www.kodakgallery.co.uk

Snapfish at www.snapfish.com

Winkflash at www.winkflash.com

Kodak at www.kodakgallery.com

Hot tip

If you use Kodak Easyshare software, you can use it for direct access to the Kodak online site shown here.

Creating Albums

Once you have chosen a photo sharing site and registered, the first thing to do is to create your own albums into which you can copy photos from your own computer, before you start sharing them. To do this:

Don't forget

Numerous albums can be created within your own sharing area.

Beware

Most online sites have a limit on the photos you can store. The restriction is on the total file size of the photos being stored on the site.

1 Click on the Create New Album icon

My Albums
Choose an album to view

Create
New Album

2 The options for creating the album are displayed

Upload Photos
Upload photos to a new album.

Album title: My New Album
Album date: March ▼ 4 ▼ 2009 ▼
Description:

Picture title ☐ Use filenames as photo titles.
Continue

3 Enter the details for the album, such as the name and the date on which it was created

Album title: World tour
Album date: March ▼ 4 ▼ 2009 ▼

Description: Photos from around the globe

4 Click Continue to move to the next step

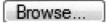

5 Click the Browse button to navigate to photos on your own computer

6 Select a photo that you want to upload into your online album

Hot tip

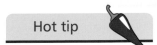

Some sites have a Quick Upload option where the contents of a whole folder can be uploaded, without having to select the photos individually.

7 Click the Open button

...cont'd

8 Repeat the selection process until you have selected all of the photos that you want to include

Pictures selected: 4

- ☐ detail1.jpg
- ☐ boats1.jpg
- ☐ terracotta1.jpg
- ☐ great_wall2.jpg

9 Click the Upload button to start uploading the photos

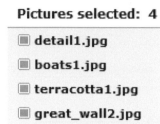

10 As the photos are being uploaded an information window tells you what is happening. The uploading can take a few minutes, depending on the speed of the Internet connection being used and the number and size of the photos

Don't forget

Individual photos and whole albums can be edited or deleted after they have been created.

11 Once the uploading has been completed, the selected photos are visible in the newly created album

My Albums > 2009 > World tour

World tour
March 4, 2009 (4 photos)

Photos from around the globe

Options ▾   Options ▾

Sharing Photos

When photos have been uploaded into an album on the online sharing site, it is then possible to make this album visible to anyone you want, e.g. members of your family and close friends. To do this:

1 Click on the Share Photos tab at the top of your homepage within the online sharing site

| View & Edit Photos | Share Photos |

2 The page displays the albums that you have created. These are the ones that you can now share with family and friends

2009 Albums **Create a new album**

World tour2
3/4/09 (4 photos)
Select album

World tour1
3/4/09 (1 photo)
Select album

3 Click the Select Album button to select an album for sharing with other people

World tour2
3/4/09 (4 photos)
Select album

Beware

On some sharing sites, people will have to register to view photos once they have been invited. This is the same registration process as for joining the site in the first place.

159

...cont'd

4 The selected album will be marked as ready to be shared

World tour2
3/4/09 (4 photos)
✓ This album will be shared

5 Click the Next button to move to the next step

Next ▶

6 Enter the details of the person, or people, with whom you want to share the album. This includes their email address and a message to go in the accompanying email

To: eilidhvandome@mac.com,lucyvandome@mac.com

Separate addresses with commas or semicolons, or select addresses from Friends & Groups.

Subject: My World Tour!

Message: You're invited to view my online photos at the Gallery. Enjoy!

7 Click the Send Invitation button to invite the selected person, or people, to view your album

Send Invitation ▶

8 Confirmation appears that the album has been shared

Your album has been shared

You'll soon receive a copy of the email that was sent to your friends.
Please visit your Guestbook to see who has viewed your album and left comments.

View Slideshow

❖ Share this slideshow again
❖ Create a new share

11 Getting Prints

This chapter details the options for printing digital photos at home, in store or online.

Options for Printing

In the early days of consumer digital photography, obtaining good quality prints was a considerable issue. The price was relatively high and the quality relatively poor. However, this has changed dramatically, to the point where it is now possible to get excellent quality prints, at good value, from a variety of sources. The main ways are:

- **Printing at home**. This can be done with a photo-quality inkjet printer. These are inexpensive and can give very good results. Their one drawback is that the price of the ink for these printers can be high, but you only print the photos that you want

- **Retail stores**. Most consumer photographic retailers now have facilities for printing digital photos, from memory cards, CDs or most removable storage devices. The quality can be comparable to that of film prints and, as you can select which photos are to be printed, the cost is very competitive. You can get your photos in a variety of sizes, up to poster size, and it is also sometimes possible to get photos printed onto items such as T-shirts, mugs and even cakes

- **Online printing services**. The development of digital photography has resulted in a corresponding growth in online printing services. To use these, you send the photos via the Web to the online service provider, who then prints the photos and sends them back via traditional mail. Again, this provides excellent quality prints and it is a great way to get hard copies without having to leave the comfort of your own home

- **Photo printers**. One printing innovation in recent years has been photo printers. These are printers that can print photos directly from a memory card or from the camera, without the photos having to be downloaded onto a computer first. Some also have the facility to crop photos and adjust color and red-eye before they are printed. These devices are either inkjet printers or a type called dye-sublimation printers

Printing Photos at Home

In some ways, printing photos at home on a photo-quality inkjet printer gives you the most flexibility: you can edit the photos on your computer first and then print them out at a specific size. There are two ways in which photos can be printed on a home photo-quality inkjet printer:

Using the operating system

If you are using Windows, photos can be printed directly, without having to open them first. To do this:

1 Access Pictures, navigate to the required folder of photos and click on one photo to select it

butterfly1

2 Click on the Print button

...cont'd

3 The Photo Printing Wizard appears. This will guide you through the printing process

4 Click the Options link

Options...

5 The Print Settings window has options for printing the photo, such as sharpening to make it crisper

Print Settings

☑ Sharpen for printing

☑ Only show options that are compatible with my printer
Certain combinations of paper type, paper size, and print quality may not print well or be available with all printers. Limiting your options to only those that are compatible will give you the best results.

Color Management...

Printer Properties...

OK   Cancel

6 Click the Printer Properties link

Printer Properties...

Beware

Make sure that you select the correct photos for printing. If you select the wrong ones, it could be expensive in terms of wasted ink and paper.

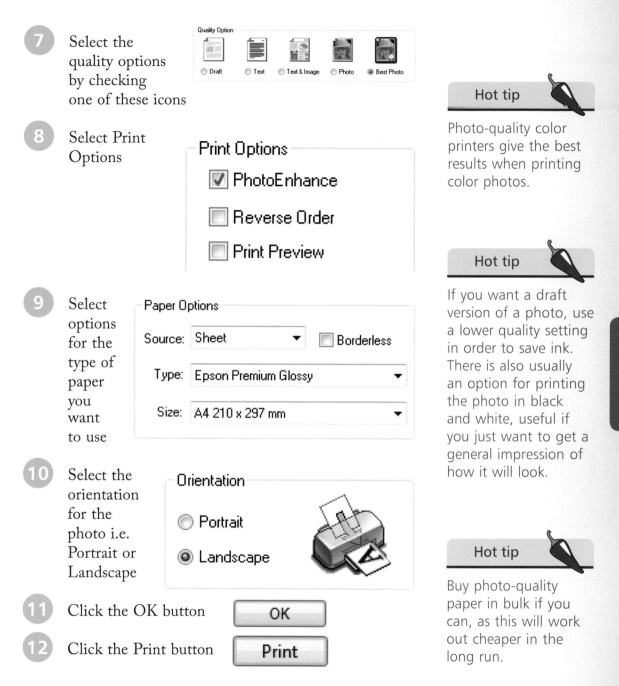

7 Select the quality options by checking one of these icons

8 Select Print Options

9 Select options for the type of paper you want to use

10 Select the orientation for the photo i.e. Portrait or Landscape

11 Click the OK button

12 Click the Print button

Hot tip

Photo-quality color printers give the best results when printing color photos.

Hot tip

If you want a draft version of a photo, use a lower quality setting in order to save ink. There is also usually an option for printing the photo in black and white, useful if you just want to get a general impression of how it will look.

Hot tip

Buy photo-quality paper in bulk if you can, as this will work out cheaper in the long run.

...cont'd

Using photo editing software

Another option for printing photos from your own computer is to use a photo editing program. This can give you more flexibility as far as the formatting of the photo is concerned. To do this, using Photoshop Elements:

 Access the Organizer section, select a photo and select File>Print from the Menu bar

2 Select the printer and the size at which you want your print produced

3 Select the type of print (this can be individual, contact sheet or picture package)

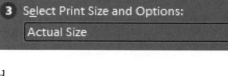

4 Select the size at which you want the prints produced

5 Click on the Add button to place more photos in the print dialog window

6 Select the location from where you want to add photos

7 Check on the boxes next to the photos you want to add to the print dialog window

8 Click the Done button

...cont'd

9 Under Type of Print, select the Contact Sheet option

10 This creates a print with thumbnails of all of the selected photos

Printing with a photo editing program enables you to be more creative with the way in which photos are arranged and printed.

168

11 Under Type of Print, select the Picture Package option

12 This enables you to print different photos on the same page

13 Click the Print button

In-store Printing

A lot of photographic retail stores now have photo kiosks which can be used to select photos and send them for printing. These kiosks can be used in a self-service way, or shop assistants will be happy to offer advice and help with using the kiosks. To print photos from a photo kiosk in a retail store:

1 Insert the media on which the photos are stored into the photo kiosk (this can be the camera's memory card, a CD, a floppy disk or a removable pen drive)

2 Select the photos that you want printed

Don't forget

Photo kiosks can also be used to print photos that have been taken on mobile phones.

169

3 Select the number of prints for each photo (there is no limit to the number of copies that can be made from a photo)

4 Select the size of print

5 Send the photos to the printer

6 The photos will then be printed and delivered, just like prints from a film

Printing Photos Online

Online printing services are an excellent way to get good value, good quality prints without having to move away from your computer. There are dozens of these services available and they can either be accessed directly on the Web (try entering "online printing" into Google) or, for Windows users, from a link within Windows. Either way, you will have to register for the online site before you can start ordering prints (see Chapter Ten, page 153, for details of registering for an online sharing/printing service). To order prints from an online service:

(see Chapter Ten, page 153, for details of registering for an online sharing/printing service)

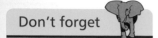

Don't forget

For Mac users, prints can be ordered online using the iPhoto program.

1 Access your chosen online printing site and log in

2 Click the Buy Prints link

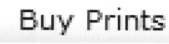

3 Select an existing album within your site

Hot tip

It is free to register for an online printing service and in some cases you get a number of free prints when you register.

World tour2
3/4/09 (4 photos)

170

4   Select the size of print required and the quantity

Item 1: Frame it | Create cards				Remove
	Size:		Price:	Quantity:
	Wallets		Sale $1.59	0
	4 x 6"		$0.15	1
	5 x 7"		Sale $0.84	0
4 x 6" Adjust Cropping	8 x 10"		Sale $2.99	0
	16 x 20" **		Sale $14.99	0
	20 x 30" **		Sale $18.99	0

5   Select the type of paper you would like used

Paper Finish

⦿ Glossy   ◯ Matte

Glossy and matte choices available for Prints up to 8x10, Collages up to 8x10, Stickers and Print Cards.

6   Select a border style for the prints (optional)

Borders

☐ Thin White   ☐ Sloppy Thin

7   Click the Checkout button to proceed to a secure area for paying for your prints

Checkout ▶

Printing Without a Computer

Although home printing on an inkjet printer is a flexible and feasible option it is not ideal for everyone, particularly those who are not comfortable working with downloading and editing photos on a computer. One way around this is to use a self-contained photo printer. These are printers that can print photos directly from the camera's memory card or the camera itself, without the need to first download the photos onto a computer. There are two main types of photo printers:

Inkjets

These are inkjet printers that can have memory cards inserted directly into them. Most printers of this type will be able to use all of the different types of memory card on the market, so you do not have to worry about buying a camera with a specific type of memory card.

There is usually a facility for some limited editing, such as cropping and color adjustment, and then the photos can be printed directly from the memory card. In general, inkjet photo printers are more expensive than those that do not offer the facility of printing directly from a memory card. These printers should not be confused with photo-quality inkjet printers, which print photos directly from a computer.

Dedicated camera printers

These are printers that connect directly to the camera (usually by the camera sitting on top of the printer as it would on a docking station – see page 24); the photos can be downloaded directly to the printer. The photos are printed using a method of dye-sublimation which puts a continuous coating of ink on the paper as opposed to the individual dots that are used with an inkjet printer. This produces a very good quality of print but the maximum size is usually restricted to 6 inches by 4 inches.

A lot of manufacturers, such as Kodak, Canon and Sony, have their own dedicated printers that work with their respective brands of cameras.

12 Displaying and Keeping

Everyone loves looking at digital photos. This chapter shows some creative ways in which photos can be displayed and stored.

Creating Family Slide Shows

One of the most satisfying aspects of digital photographs is being able to display them to family and friends. One way of doing this is to create slide shows that can then be viewed on a computer or a television. This can be done in two ways:

Within Windows

For Windows users, slide shows can be created within the Windows operating system. However, these can only be viewed on the computer. To do this:

1 Click the Start button

2 Click on the Pictures button

Pictures

3 Double-click on a folder in Pictures to open it

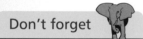

Don't forget

If required, a folder can be selected and then viewed as a slide show. This will automatically display all of the photos in that folder.

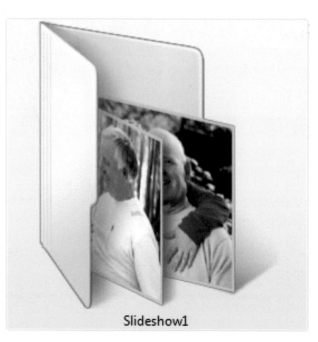

Slideshow1

4 If desired, select individual photos to include in the slide show. If none are selected, all of the photos will be included

5 Click on the Slide Show button

6 All of the selected photos are displayed as a slide show

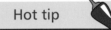 Hot tip

Slide shows such as the one on this page can be displayed on a television, but only if the computer is first connected to it.

7 Use these controls to move through the slide show, pause it, go to the beginning or the end and select options for its appearance

...cont'd

Using a photo editing program

In some ways, a better option is to create a slide show with a photo editing program. The advantage of this is that it can be saved as a self-contained presentation and then copied onto a CD so that it can be viewed in more comfort on a television, rather than just on a computer. To do this, using Photoshop Elements:

176

1 Open one, or more, images in the Editor or select them in the Organizer

2 In either the Editor or the Organizer, click on the Create button

CREATE

3 Click on the Slide Show button

Slide Show...

4 Select options for how you want the Slide Show to operate, such as slide duration, type of transition between slides and background music. Click on the OK button

---

Slide Show Preferences   ×

Slide Show Default Options

Static Duration: 5 sec

Transition: Fade

Transition Duration: 2 sec

Background Color: ■

☐ Apply Pan & Zoom to All Slides

✔ Include Photo Captions as Text

✔ Include Audio Captions as Narration

✔ Repeat Soundtrack Until Last Slide

Crop to Fit Slide: ☐ Landscape Photos   ☐ Portrait Photos

Preview Playback Options

Preview Quality: High

✔ Show this dialog each time a new Slide Show is created.

OK   Cancel

5   The main Slide
     Show window is
     displayed

 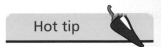
6   Use these
     buttons to
     preview the whole Slide Show

7   The images and
     transitions are displayed
     in the timeline. Click
     on a transition box to
     select a different one

8   Use these buttons to add
     graphics, text and narration
     to the Slide Show

9   Set the duration for each slide and also whether
     panning and tilting is enabled for when the Slide
     Show is viewed

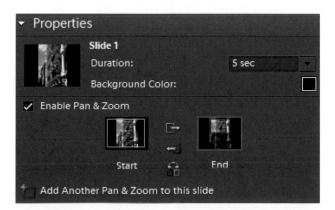

...cont'd

 10 Click on the Add Media button to add more content to the Slide Show

+ Add Media ▾

Photos and Videos from Organizer...
Photos and Videos from Folder...

Audio from Organizer...
Audio from Folder...

11 Click on the Add Blank Slide button if you want to  include a blank slide. This can then have content added to it in the same way as text and graphics and be used in a variety of ways, such as a title page for the Slide Show

12 Click on the Save Project button to save the file as a project. This can then be opened from the Organizer and edited

13 Click on the Output button so that the Slide Show can be saved in a format that can be shared

14 The Slide Show Output window has options for saving the Slide Show

15 Select the use to which you want to put the Slide Show

16 Select the file type for how you want to save the Slide Show

17 Click on the OK button to save the Slide Show in the selected file format. This can be used to display the Slide Show and also share it with other people

Saving Family Slide Shows

Once a slide show has been created it can then be saved onto a CD so that it can be displayed on another computer or a television. To save it onto a CD, using Photoshop Elements:

1 Select a Slide Show project in the Organizer

2 Click on the Create button

3 Select More Options and click on the VCD with Menu button

4 The Slide Show selected in Step 1 is displayed in the Create a VCD with Menu window

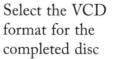

5 If you want to include another Slide Show, click on the Add Slide Shows button and select another from the Organizer

6 Select the VCD format for the completed disc

7 Click on the Burn button to create the VCD

Burn...

Digital Cards

Using a photo editing program such as Photoshop Elements it is possible to produce digital greetings cards or postcards. These can then be printed or sent to people electronically by email. To do this:

 1 Open a photo you want to use in a card

 Don't forget

Most online printing services have an option for printing cards, but these are usually in large quantities. If you just want a small number it is probably more cost-effective to do it yourself.

2 Click on the Create button

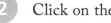

3 Click on the Greeting Card button

...cont'd

4 Select a theme for the look of the card

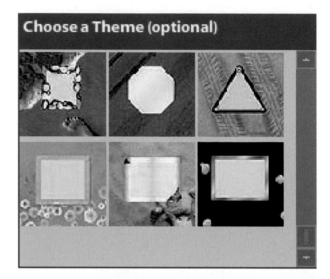

Don't forget

Depending on the type of card being created, you may only be able to select one photo for it – e.g. for a postcard. However, for folded cards, you may be able to select several photos for the card.

5 Select a layout for the way the photo appears in the card

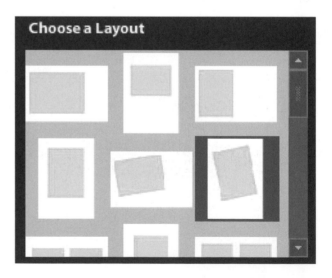

6 Click on the Done button

7 The selected theme or layout is applied to the photo

8 The photo is added to the card template

9 Add text to the card in the same way as you would for any other image

10 Save the card in the same way as any other photo

Viewing from a CD or DVD

In the digital world, digital photographs are frequently saved onto CDs or DVDs. This is an efficient and secure way of saving photos and it also means that photos can easily be transferred from one computer to another. If you are given a CD or DVD containing photos the essential thing is to be able to view them. To do this:

1 Place the CD or DVD in the appropriate drive in the computer

2 The computer should recognize the disc and offer options for viewing. Select an option, such as "Open folder to view files," and click OK

3 If the disc dialog box does not launch automatically click Start and then Computer. The disc will be shown as a separate drive. Double-click on the disc to open it

4 The contents of the disc are displayed within the normal interface and the photos can be viewed in the usual way

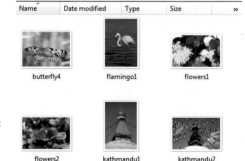

The Value of Backing Up

Backing up is the process of creating a copy of your important files so that they are safe in the event of a major accident occurring to your computer, such as fire or theft. If you do not have a backup of your files they could be lost permanently – including your precious photos. Backing up should be seen as general housekeeping and be done as regularly as possible, approximately once every couple of weeks. Some points to bear in mind about backing up:

- It is a chore, but one that could be invaluable. It is a bit like paying for insurance: you hope you never have to use it, but if you do, you are glad you went to the effort

- Back up your files onto some form of removable storage such as a CD or a DVD (external hard drives can be used but they are not as secure because they will probably be located near to the computer – see below). Pen drives are another option for backing up digital photos

- Store your backup copies away from the computer from which they came – if there is an accident such as a fire, you do not want your backups perishing in the same way as the computer. If possible, keep your backups in a separate physical location from the computer

- Some companies on the Web offer online storage where you upload your photos onto their servers, where the photos are stored. However, there is usually a fee for this and there can be issues if the company goes bust or has problems with their servers

- Get into the habit of backing up regularly, particularly after you have downloaded new photos onto your computer. Ideally, enter a recurring reminder into a calendar on your computer

- Always expect the worst – then it will probably never happen, but if it does you will be prepared and hopefully your photos will be preserved

Burning CDs and DVDs

There are programs for saving files to CD or DVD, but this can also be done directly within Windows. To do this:

1 Open Pictures and select the images that you want to save to CD or DVD

Name	Date modified	Type	Size	Tags

big_ben1   hong_kong_night1

2 Click on the Burn button on the folder toolbar

3 Enter a name for the disc

Burn a Disc

Prepare this blank disc

Disc title: Vacations

Show formatting options   Next   Cancel

4 Click on the Next button to format the disc and burn the selected files onto it

Next

Index